Rosalind Niblett has lived in Hertfordshire for most of her life. After graduating from Cardiff University she directed excavations at Colchester and was then County Archaeologist for Buckinghamshire. Since 1978 she has lived and worked in St Albans, where she has conducted many excavations, including that of the royal burial, which she discovered in 1992. She has published many articles and excavation reports, and also a book on the Trinovantes in the Peoples of Roman Britain series. She is a member of the Institute of Field Archaeologists and a Fellow of the Society of Antiquaries.

Following page
Fig. 1 The Verulamium Venus, a 21cm high bronze statuette of Venus
that was waiting to be melted down in a box of scrap metal
in a 2nd century bronze-worker's shop in Verulamium.
(Copyright St Albans Museums)

ROMAN HERTFORDSHIRE

Rosalind Niblett

DOVECOTE PRESS

First published in 1995 by The Dovecote Press Ltd
Stanbridge, Wimborne, Dorset BH21 4JD

ISBN 1 874336 34 2

© Rosalind Niblett 1995

Photoset in Sabon by The Typesetting Bureau,
Wimborne, Dorset
Printed and bound by Biddles Ltd,
Guildford & Kings Lynn

1 3 5 7 8 6 4 2

Contents

Acknowledgements

A large number of people have helped me write this book, and I am glad of the opportunity to thank them. Stuart Bryant, Gil Burleigh, David Neal, Wendy Parry, Tony Rook, Chris Saunders and Simon West have commented on the text, and patiently provided answers to many questions. Acknowledgements and thanks are also due to the St Albans Museums Service for permission to reproduce many of the illustrations, including those on the front and back covers, to the British Museum for Figs. 5, 6, 47, and 49, to Stuart Bryant for Figs. 35 and 36, to the Cambridge University Committee for Aerial Photography for Fig. 30, to the Hertfordshire Archaeological Trust for Figs. 35 and 36, to the Mill Green Museum Hatfield for Figs. 40 and 51, to David Neal for Fig. 38, to the North Herts Museum Service for Figs. 4, 28, 32, 53, 58 and the back cover, and to Simon West for Fig. 56. The estate of the late Alan Sorrell kindly gave permission to reproduce the reconstructions for the front cover and Fig. 16. With the exception of Fig. 59 which was drawn by Clare Pollak, all the line illustrations are the work of Alex Thorne. Finally particular thanks go to my husband Robert for sustained and patient help, not least with the Latin translations.

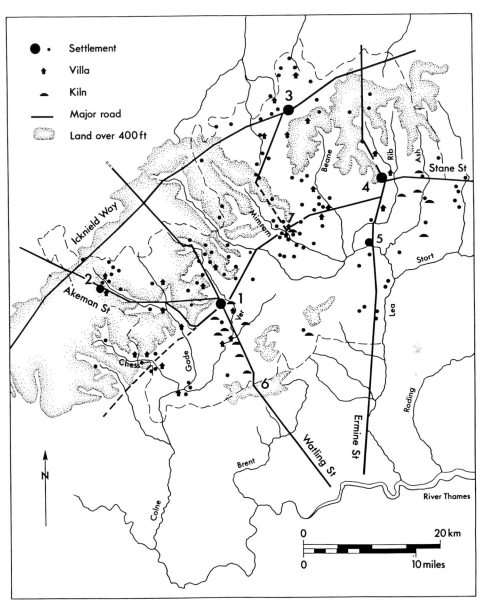

Hertfordshire in the Roman period. 1 Verulamium; 2 Cow Roast; 3 Baldock;
4 Braughing; 5 Ware; 6 Elstree; 7 Welwyn. *(Drawn by Alex Thorne).*

Hertfordshire before the Romans

The county of Hertfordshire is an artificial creation of the late Saxon period, with boundaries that were determined by the military and administrative requirements of the time. Until then, the concept of Hertfordshire would have had no meaning.

Although Hertfordshire is densely populated, there remains a surprisingly large area of countryside. Nevertheless it is difficult now to imagine the landscape of the first century BC. Amid the urban sprawls of the late twentieth century, it is all too easy to forget the physical structure which moulded the early development of the area which now forms the county.

Broadly speaking, Hertfordshire consists of three main zones. To the north and west lies the steep chalk escarpment of the Chiltern Hills, with a sloping plateau falling away to the south and east. Except for a small area in the north, this plateau is largely overlain by clay with flints, produced by the gradual weathering of the chalk. By contrast much of south-east Hertfordshire is covered by London Clay, while the north-east of the county forms part of a large area of Boulder Clay which was originally laid down beneath ice sheets during the Ice Age. Over most of the county the drainage is dominated by two main river systems. In the north, the rivers Rib, Beane, Ashe and Mimram drain into the Lea which ultimately joins the Thames at London (Blackwall). Further south, the rivers of the central Chilterns, the Ver, Gade, Misbourne and Chess, are tributaries of the Colne which meets the Thames at Staines.

These differences in surface geology have produced rather different soils. For early farmers the soils on the more mixed Boulder Clay were easier to cultivate than the acid soils on the Chiltern slopes and the heavy London Clay. The river valleys have cut through deposits of sand and gravel, which were originally laid down by streams running south from the edge of melting glaciers. Here the resulting soils are lighter, and together with the chalk escarpment, formed the most attractive areas in the county for prehistoric settlement.

Nevertheless, man's early settlement was not confined to these areas, and by the middle of the first century BC Hertfordshire was comparatively well populated. By the standards of the time, the sand and gravels of the Colne river system seem to have been intensively farmed. Grains of pollen, preserved in the peat and silts of the flood plain of the Ver, suggest that in this valley at least, the primeval forest cover had long since been replaced by pasture and cornland. By contrast, the heavy clays over much of south-east Hertfordshire may have remained well-wooded right up to the time of the Roman conquest and beyond.

THE PEOPLE

In the century immediately before the Roman conquest Hertfordshire was occupied by groups of late Iron Age people growing cereal crops and raising sheep, cattle and horses. Hertfordshire at the time was far from being a backwater. The steady expansion of the Roman Empire during the first century BC resulted in successive waves of refugees from the Continent crossing to southern Britain, and Hertfordshire was on the receiving end of a constant stream of new stimuli and processes. Highly skilled iron and bronze smiths produced not only serviceable tools and weapons, but also, on occasion, richly decorated items with abstract curvilinear designs, often inlaid with enamel. Spindle whorls and clay weights from upright looms bear witness to the production of woven cloth, while the introduction of the potter's wheel and new firing techniques allowed the production of fine, wheel-turned vessels, although entirely hand-finished pots also continued to be made. Trade increased as new markets opened up in Roman Gaul, while the organisation of society seems to have become progressively more centralised, particularly during the first century AD.

We know something of the people themselves from the works of Greek and Roman writers. Along with the other inhabitants of England (and France) at the time, they were Celts, speaking a language ancestral to Welsh, Gaelic, Irish and Cornish. They were organised into clans or tribal groups, and the flamboyant lifestyle of their leaders caught the attention of the Greek geographer,

Strabo, who considered them 'passionately devoted to war, excitable and always ready to fight, but in other respects straightforward and not lacking in culture.' This description is borne out by a Roman writer, Ammianus Marcellinus, who described the Celts as 'very tall, blond and red faced; fierce-looking with glaring eyes, always fighting, very proud and aggressive.'

Perhaps the most informative source on the Celts at this period is Julius Caesar, who described their customs at some length. He tells us that 'in Celtic society the common people are almost like slaves; there are two kinds of men who have any importance and status. One of these is the Druids and the other the knights. The Druids are concerned with religion, controlling public and private sacrifices and determining ritual. Many young men come to them for instruction, treating them with great respect. The Druids decide almost all public and private disputes. They judge crimes and murders, and settle disagreements about inheritance or boundaries. The Druids do not take part in war. The knights however all go out to fight whenever a war breaks out (as happened almost every year until Caesar's intervention). The highest-born and wealthiest knights are followed into battle by the greatest number of bondsmen and clients. This is the only way in which they measure their power and status.'

The system of clientship was a particularly important bond that held society together and probably persisted at least until the late Roman period. Under this system a wealthier or more powerful patron would support and protect a number of clients in return for services or produce. The other important social class, that of the Druids, was responsible not simply for religious matters, but also for the whole body of traditional learning, music, poetry, mathematics and law. Although the power of this class must certainly have diminished in the Roman period, there is no reason to suppose that Druids completely died out. There are still occasional references to them in the literature of late Roman Gaul.

Archaeologists have not yet excavated many Hertfordshire sites that were occupied in the first century BC, but those which are known demonstrate a rather different aspect of Celtic society. Although people whom Caesar would have classed as Druids and knights no doubt lived here, the local Celts were predominantly farmers, living in extended family groups in small settlements, surrounded by fields, droveways and cattle enclosures.

[11]

Julius Caesar first landed on the coast of Kent in 55 BC, but it was not until his return in the late summer of the following year that he was able to penetrate far enough inland to reach Hertfordshire. His progress had forced the local British tribes to take the unusual, and no doubt unwelcome step of combining under a single leader. By the time Caesar and his army had marched some 80 miles and had reached a fordable point on the Thames, this leader, a chieftain named Cassivellaunus, had been chosen as overall commander of the British resistance.

Caesar defeated Cassivellaunus at the Thames crossing, but not in finally crushing him. In order to do so the Romans had to push still further inland, and in his memoirs Caesar described the events of the late summer of 54 BC in his usual terse prose. 'Our army pressed on, laying waste, burning and plundering. In this however, we were severely hampered by the native forces who all the time were hiding in the woods and harrying any of the Roman forces who strayed away from the main body. They had 4,000 charioteers which they used to swoop down on any stragglers. They had also rounded up and driven away a very large quantity of cattle, so there was less for us to plunder.'

Caesar's account of his troubles north of the Thames, perhaps somewhere in the Lea valley, is our earliest description of Hertfordshire and its inhabitants. The countryside was obviously well populated and had sufficient pasture to support cattle, as well as the horses needed to draw the war chariots. At the same time there was plenty of surviving woodland which provided cover for the guerrilla tactics employed by the local people.

Although he does not admit this directly, it is clear that Caesar had considerable difficulty in achieving his main objective, that of finding the place which Cassivellaunus was using as his stronghold. In the end he only succeeded with help from some of the Celtic tribes who had given up their resistance. Once located however, the base was quickly overwhelmed, and a final, crushing defeat was inflicted on Cassivellaunus. Terms were then arranged whereby Cassivellaunus agreed to give hostages, to pay an annual tribute to Rome, and to refrain from molesting the neighbouring Trinovantes, who occupied land in what today is Essex and Suffolk. Until recently they had been the most powerful local tribe, but this had changed when Cassivellaunus killed their king and

Fig.2. The Devil's Dyke, Wheathampstead; part of the defences of a pre-Roman stronghold dating from the 1st century BC. *(Copyright St Albans Museums)*.

forced their young prince Mandubracius to flee for his life. Mandubracius had placed himself under Caesar's protection and was now restored as part of the terms of the treaty. As soon as the treaty had been agreed, Caesar returned to Gaul, taking his army with him. He never crossed to Britain again.

Archaeologists have so far been unable to add very much to Caesar's account of what must have been a traumatic summer for the people of Hertfordshire. Even the site of Cassivellaunus' stronghold is unknown, although various suggestions have been made. Caesar describes it as defended by banks and ditches and concealed among woods and swamps. Large numbers of cattle had been driven into the stronghold for safety, implying that the defences encompassed a substantial amount of land. Many years ago Sir Mortimer Wheeler suggested that Cassivellaunus' base may have lain to the west of the modern village of Wheathampstead in the upper Lea valley. Here part of a massive bank and ditch still survives as a formidable earthwork known as Devil's Dyke (fig. 2). The ditch, originally 40 feet deep in places, formed the south-west side of a 100 acre enclosure whose northern and eastern sides were marked by natural valleys and marshy land. In these respects Wheathampstead fits Caesar's description very well, but unfortunately excavations here have so far not provided any supporting evidence to show conclusively that this is indeed the site described by Caesar. Many archaeologists now think that the final battle between Caesar and Cassivellaunus probably took place elsewhere.

Other possible sites are equally problematic. Ravensburgh Castle, at the head of the Mimram valley in north Hertfordshire, is a 17 acre site defended by banks and ditches. Although wooded, it lies on the crest of the chalk escarpment and can hardly be described as swampy, even after prolonged rain. The summer of 54 BC seems to have been an exceptionally dry one; the harvest in northern France was very poor that year due to a severe drought. So for this reason if none other Ravensburgh seems an unlikely candidate. Two other possible sites in Hertfordshire are the hill forts at Redbourn (west of St Albans) (fig. 3) and at Gatesbury

Fig.3. Aerial view of the Aubreys, an Iron Age hill fort on the south-west side of Redbourn. *(Copyright St Albans Museums).*

(near Braughing). Both are defended by banks and ditches, both are in areas that may have been wooded in the first century BC, and both are only slightly raised above low-lying, marshy ground. Unfortunately neither can be firmly dated to the invasion period. Both these hill forts and the one at Ravensburgh may well belong to a much earlier period. In the absence of firm information, Cassivellaunus' stronghold remains as elusive to us as it was to Caesar.

Cassivellaunus himself is also a shadowy figure. He was probably the warlord of a small tribal group, one of the many which seem to have occupied south-east Britain at the time. Caesar names five tribes who surrendered to him north of the Thames and gave away the location of Cassivellaunus' stronghold: the Cenimagni, the Segontiaci, the Ancalites, the Bibroci and the Cassi. The Cenimagni have been identified as the Iceni of Norfolk, and it has been suggested that the Segontiaci were in fact based south of the Thames, but the remaining three tribes may well have had territory in Hertfordshire. On the grounds of the similarity of the names, it seems eminently likely that the Cassi were the tribe to which Cassivellaunus himself belonged, but the extent of their territory is totally unknown.

From Invasion to Conquest

After Caesar's departure no Roman army set foot in Britain for 97 years, years which saw unprecedented changes in the Hertfordshire area. First and foremost, there was a dramatic increase in foreign trade. It looks as if Caesar's exploits, in a land which up until then most Mediterranean people had viewed as semi-mythical, encouraged enterprising traders to follow in his wake. Up until about 50 BC, trade between Celtic Britain and the Continent had been via communities on the south coast of England and their counterparts in Brittany. After Caesar's expeditions the trade routes shifted north with traders from north Gaul pushing up the Thames and Lea. Both rivers were almost certainly navigable at the time, at any rate for flat-bottomed boats, and it is in the rich pasture lands of east and central Hertfordshire that the first fruits of increased foreign trade can be seen.

A generation after Caesar's departure an important trading post was thriving on the banks of the River Rib. Today the site lies on the outskirts of the village of Braughing, 7 miles north of Ware. The area had first been settled by groups of farmers some centuries previously, and at some stage a defended site had been established on the hill overlooking the river at Gatesbury. Then in about 30 BC the settlement expanded dramatically, to cover some 300 acres across the valley floor and around Wickham Hill. Although it is doubtful whether all this area was occupied at any one time, a substantial settlement clearly developed. By the last quarter of the century, large quantities of imported goods were reaching Braughing; more Italian and Gaulish pottery of this date has been found here than anywhere else in either Hertfordshire or Essex.

Another important centre grew up 12 miles to the north-west at Baldock. This settlement lay on the Icknield Way, and also commanded an important trade route through the Chilterns by way of the Hitchin Gap. Early in the first century BC Baldock was the home of a group of wealthy Celtic aristocrats; several rich graves

Fig.4. A bronze bound bucket from a 'chieftain's grave' at Baldock. 1st century BC. *(Copyright North Herts District Council Museums Service).*

have been excavated, including two chieftain's burials (fig. 4). By the end of the century the settlement covered several square miles and was made up of a network of farmsteads, cemeteries, fields, stockyards and droveways. The whole complex was defined by a number of formidable earthworks in the form of impressive banks and ditches. Further south, thriving settlements with rich burials, traces of domestic occupation, and substantial earthworks are known or suspected at Welches Farm, Welwyn and Welwyn Garden City.

The geographer Strabo, who wrote at the end of the first century BC, tells us that the principal exports from Britain to the Roman world were silver, iron, cattle, corn, hides, hunting dogs and slaves. We have already seen that large numbers of cattle were reared in Hertfordshire, and these would have provided hides, while corn, iron and hunting dogs were doubtless also produced locally. Since the inter-tribal feuding that seems to have been a constant feature of Celtic life would have guaranteed a ready supply of slaves, silver is the only item on Strabo's list of exports that could not have been produced in the county.

In return for these exports, luxury goods suitable for feasting and drinking were brought into Hertfordshire: Italian wine in large wine jars (*amphorae*), fine tableware from Italy and Gaul, and ornate silverware like the splendid cups from a grave at Welwyn (fig. 5). In time these exotic objects were placed as offerings in the graves of the powerful and well-to-do. Nearly a dozen richly equipped graves are known from the county. They are concentrated in central and northern Hertfordshire, particularly in the Welwyn and Welwyn Garden City area, and span a period of about 100 years. All the grave offerings reflect a love of feasting, together with a desire to display lavish and luxurious possessions, and confirm the observations of classical writers who were unanimous in their description of the Celts as a people who loved feasting and extravagant personal display.

Richly equipped graves however must have belonged to an aristocratic elite, exploiting its ability to control the newly opened trade routes with the Roman world. For the ordinary people, life must have been very much more mundane. Settlements at this period usually consisted of farmsteads, sometimes in small groups, sometimes more isolated. They were surrounded by networks of ditched stockpens, droveways and small square or rectangular fields. The buildings themselves were invariably wooden, and either round or rectangular in plan. Some settlements such as one

Fig.5. Two silver cups from a 'chieftain's grave' at Welwyn. (*Copyright British Museum*).

from Park Street, near Radlett, were probably only occupied by a single family, and allowing for dependants and servants probably did not exceed 40 or 50 people at the most. Others, such as Baldock, Wheathampstead or Welwyn, covered many acres and must have been occupied by rather larger communities.

Although most settlements were purely agricultural, by the early first century AD a few had started specialising in various industrial activities. At Welwyn pottery kilns were established, producing fine wheel-made pottery imitating forms current on the Continent. At Northchurch, west of Berkhamsted, an important iron working industry grew up, which ultimately extended over about 4 square miles. Iron ore occurs naturally in the clay of the valley floor and, by the time of the Roman conquest, most of the iron used in Hertfordshire was probably smelted here. Even in their heyday, however, none of these settlements was ever a town in the modern sense of the word.

A feature of these late Iron Age settlements is their apparently peaceful character. Admittedly many of the farmsteads were surrounded by deep ditches and earth banks, but these seem to have been constructed more to prevent livestock straying than for defence. It is only occasionally that chance discoveries of chariot fittings or fragments of swords, scabbards and spears remind us of the warlike nature of the warrior aristocracy that held sway before the Roman conquest, and which bear out Strabo's remark that the Celts were a nation 'passionately devoted to war' (fig. 6).

Fig.6. Bronze and iron lynch pin. Used to prevent a chariot wheel slipping off the axle. Found at Kings Langley. (*Copyright British Museum*).

By the second half of the first century BC gold, silver and bronze coins were being produced in increasing amounts in south-east Britain. These were probably used more to advertise a ruler's wealth and prestige than as currency in the modern sense. The first coins minted in Hertfordshire were not inscribed with any name, but carried designs, based ultimately on those current in the Graeco-Roman world. Who was responsible for minting these early coins we do not know, but presumably they were the leaders of the various tribal groups that occupied the area in the first century BC. On the basis of differences in the coins it has been suggested that there were at least two main tribal groups in Hertfordshire at this time. One was centred in the Chilterns in the south-west of the county, and the other in the north and east around Braughing and Baldock. Within these tribes various other sub-groups, or pagi, also existed, and it is possible that the traces of banks and ditches that still survive in the Chilterns (such as Grim's Ditch, near Tring) mark territorial divisions between these groups. Similarly the massive Beech Bottom Dyke and Devil's Ditch which can still be seen running for nearly 2 miles on the west side of St Albans, are more likely to have been territorial boundaries than defensive works. They were never continuous earthworks, and the gaps in them must once have been filled by areas of marsh or dense woodland.

We know nothing of Cassivellaunus' ultimate fate. Nor do we know how long the treaty arrangements imposed by Caesar remained in force. These had included an undertaking on the part of Cassivellaunus not to molest the Trinovantes, but as far as we know nothing was said as to the other tribes. Inter-tribal warfare seems to have been endemic before Caesar's successes in Kent forced the tribes to band together in 54 BC, and no doubt once the threat of imminent invasion by Rome had receded, raids and feuding recommenced. By the early first century AD the smaller tribes suggested by coin evidence had been replaced by a single tribe controlling not only the whole of Hertfordshire, but also areas now covered by Buckinghamshire, Oxfordshire and parts of Northamptonshire and Cambridgeshire. This tribe called itself the Catuvellauni, a Celtic name meaning good or efficient fighters. Whether this was Cassivellaunus' tribe is uncertain, but the two names are suspiciously similar.

Fig.7. Part of a clay mould from Verulamium. Used for casting the 'blanks' for coins of Cunobelin. *(Copyright St Albans Museums)*.

VERULAMIUM

In about 10 BC one tribal leader started minting coins bearing his name: Tasciovanus. He also added the name of his mint: Verulamium (modern St Albans), the town that was to become the centre for the Catuvellaunian tribe in the Roman period. Up until the early first century AD Verulamium seems to have consisted of little more than a few farmsteads, but thereafter it steadily grew in importance, gradually eclipsing Welwyn, Wheathampstead, Braughing and Baldock.

Tasciovanus ruled from about 10 BC to AD 10, when he was succeeded by Cunobelin, who was to become the most successful of all the Celtic kings of pre-Roman Britain, ultimately extending his sphere of influence over most of south-east Britain. Early in his reign Cunobelin took over the territory of the Trinovantes of Essex and south Suffolk, and moved his capital away from Verulamium to the Trinovantian centre at Camulodunum (Colchester). Nevertheless, Verulamium continued to grow in size, wealth and prestige, and coins were still minted there (fig. 7).

The Roman Conquest

Throughout his long reign Cunobelin managed to avoid serious confrontations with the Roman empire. At his death in about AD 40 he was succeeded by two sons, Togidumnus and Caratacus, who were less politically adroit, and relations with Rome quickly deteriorated. The British were accused of raiding the coast of Roman Gaul, and quarrels among the British aristocracy led one 'prince', Verica, to ask the Roman emperor for support. Events like these provided Rome with a pretext for invasion, and in the late summer of AD 43 the emperor Claudius commenced the Roman occupation of Britain.

From a Roman point of view the initial campaign progressed smoothly, and two months after the Roman army had landed at Richborough in Kent, eleven British tribes surrendered to Claudius at Cunobelin's former capital, Camulodunum. In Hertfordshire the Roman conquest did not result in widespread disruption to farms or settlements or to vast numbers of Roman soldiers being quartered on native land. On the contrary, here the conquest seems to have been a fairly 'low-key' event, and there is even evidence to suggest that the local aristocracy was able to maintain its position and traditions. One of the most dramatic archaeological discoveries in the county in recent years has been the excavation of what appears to be the burial place of a Catuvellaunian ruler. A short distance outside Verulamium itself, a large ditched enclosure was discovered during an excavation in 1992 at Folly Lane. In the centre of the enclosure was a large burial pit containing cremated human and animal bones together with a large collection of extremely expensive objects; enamelled horse equipment, a tunic of iron mail, remains of an elaborate Italian couch, and a large quantity of bronze and silver. Unfortunately nearly everything in the pit had been put on an intense fire which had melted most of the objects beyond recognition (figs. 8, 9). A few feet away from the grave pit itself was a much larger pit, over 25 feet square, in the base of which, nearly 10 feet below the

Fig.8. A bronze bridle bit and cheek piece from the royal burial at Folly Lane, Verulamium. *(Copyright St Albans Museums)*.

Fig 9. Some of the grave offerings placed in the royal burial at Folly Lane. These included fragments of horse gear (top) a chain mail tunic and bronze trumpet (left) animal remains (bottom left) and a couch and four wine jars (bottom right). *(Drawn by Alex Thorne)*.

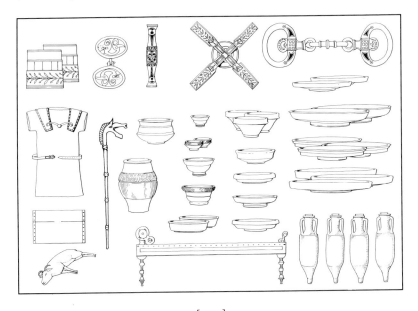

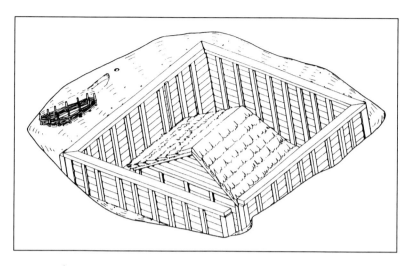

Fig. 10. The sunken chamber at Folly Lane. *(Drawn by Alex Thorne).*

ground, were the remains of a remarkable wooden chamber surrounded by a narrow 'walkway' (fig. 10). Similar, although smaller and simpler, chambers have been found at Colchester where they are thought to be funerary chambers, used during the burial rites of the ruling family. This interpretation may explain the Folly Lane example; although here the wealth and scale of the remains suggest that this ruler was someone of outstanding importance. What is more the pottery found in the Folly Lane chamber dates from shortly *after* the Roman conquest, so if this site is indeed a royal burial, it must represent someone who was able to retain his wealth and status even after the coming of Rome.

The precise identity of this ruler will never be known, but we can make a reasoned guess as to the type of person he is likely to have been. The Romans had two methods of dealing with an area they were taking over. One option was to exact tribute and then garrison the land with a network of forts; this seems to have been the method adopted in the former Trinovantian territory. Alternatively a client kingdom was established, its inhabitants disarmed, and a native leader set up as a puppet ruler, maintaining law and order and collecting tax or tribute to be paid to Rome. In return the ruler would retain his position and enjoy the protection of the Roman state. It goes without saying that such a system would only work in an area where there was a certain amount of support for Rome, but it may well be that this was the course chosen for the Hertfordshire branch of Cunobelin's old kingdom. Cunobelin's sons, Togidumnus and Caratacus, had probably divided the kingdom between them. It may be that Togidumnus' share had included the traditional Catuvellaunian lands of Hertfordshire, while Caratacus took over Trinovantian Essex and Suffolk. At all events, Togidumnus died shortly after the Romans landed. His followers, left leaderless, may well have made their peace with Rome, which then established a pro-Roman supporter as a client king.

Certainly there is no sign in Hertfordshire of pitched battles, nor of a network of Roman forts. At the time of writing, not a single fort that can definitely be assigned to the conquest period has been found in the county. The most we can point to are various items of military equipment, presumably lost by Roman soldiers, which have been found on a number of different sites. These finds include two fine Roman helmets, one probably from Verulamium and the other from Northchurch, part of a *lorica*, or body armour, from Verulamium, and a handful of javelin heads, armour fittings and slingshots from Verulamium, Northchurch, Baldock, Braughing and Enfield (fig. 11). All these sites lie on Roman roads and it seems likely that these roads mark routes used by the Roman army as it pressed north and west.

Fig.11. A Roman bronze helmet. This is on display in the Verulamium Museum, but its precise find spot is unknown. The knob on the top of the helmet once held a horsehair crest, and the projection on the left protected the wearer's neck. *(Copyright St Albans Museums)*.

Native Revolt and Roman Rule

A pro-Roman attitude among the Hertfordshire Catuvellauni at the time of the conquest led to trouble later. Neighbouring tribes, less acquiescent to Roman rule, viewed them with growing resentment, until in AD 60, matters finally came to a head. In the first century the areas that today are Norfolk and Suffolk were inhabited by the Iceni, a tribe ruled by Prasutagus, whom the Romans seem to have supported as a client king. Prasutagus died in the late 50s, at which point the Roman authorities started the process of incorporating the tribal land into the Roman province. This operation did not proceed as smoothly in Norfolk as it had done in Hertfordshire, and local resentment was fanned as stories circulated of Roman atrocities. The neighbouring Trinovantes were already smarting under a number of grievances, not least the confiscation of land which had been handed over to retired Roman soldiers based in the newly established *colonia* (a chartered town) at Camulodunum. So matters rested when in the summer of AD 60 the Roman governor, Suetonius Paulinus, departed with the bulk of the Roman army to campaign against British tribes who were still holding out in north Wales. Taking advantage of the army's absence, the Trinovantes and Iceni joined forces and rose in revolt under Prasutagus' widow, Boudicca (Boadicea), who was clearly a woman of determined character and leadership.

The rebels singled out obvious settlements of Roman supporters as their prime targets. The *colonia* at Camulodunum was their first objective and this was burnt to the ground and its inhabitants slaughtered. The rebels then pushed on to the newly established port and trading centre at London which suffered the same fate. After London they turned their attention to Verulamium.

It may be that some traditional rivalry still existed between the Trinovantes and Catuvellauni, harking right back to the time of Caesar, Cassivellaunus and Mandubracius, but there can be little doubt that the prime motive of the rebels was to destroy what seemed to them a nest of collaborators who had thrown in their lot with the Romans. The Roman historian Tacitus provides a graphic and no doubt highly coloured picture of the carnage and looting carried out in London, and it is not difficult to imagine the rebels pressing on along the newly constructed Watling Street to Verulamium to mete out further vengeance.

Archaeology cannot yet provide definite evidence for the destruction of Hertfordshire farms at this time, although at the well-to-do farmstead at Gorhambury, a mile west of Verulamium, signs of burning have been found dating from about this time. Eight miles to the north-east, a thriving farmstead at Codicote seems to have been abandoned at about this time, but whether as a direct result of the events of AD 60, is still uncertain. At Verulamium, on the other hand, there are clear traces of destruction. We shall see in a later section that Roman buildings of some pretension were already being put up in the town. All these were burnt down, and the remains of the timber and clay walls, their beaten clay floors, and the early streets and yards between them, are all cloaked with layers of burnt wattle and daub, charcoal and ash. In contrast to the situation at Colchester, where excavators have found the skulls of the unfortunate defenders thrown into the town ditch, no human victims have been discovered at Verulamium. It is possible that the inhabitants had sufficient warning of Boudicca's advance to be able to escape and seek refuge in the woods of the Chilterns. To Boudicca's followers however, rampaging across south-west Hertfordshire, it probably seemed as though the Romans were on the run.

We do not really know how long the area remained in rebel hands. Whether the events of the revolt all took place in the course of a few weeks, or whether the anarchy and chaos persisted for several months, is something that is still undecided. The Roman authorities were not prepared to give up their new province, and Boudicca must have realised that it was only a matter of time before there would have to be a final confrontation with the Roman army. In the event, the destruction of Verulamium was to prove the last of the major British successes. A detachment of the Ninth Legion had already been sent from the fortress at Lincoln in an attempt to rescue the settlers in Camulodunum, but this had been ambushed by the rebels. Even before the destruction of London word of the revolt had reached the governor Paulinus. He was unable to bring back his main force from North Wales in time to save either London or Verulamium, and Poenius Postumus, the acting commander of the Second Legion, stationed at Gloucester, had decided not to run the risk of advancing on Boudicca without reinforcements. However the deciding battle was not long delayed after the sack of Verulamium, and it may be that Boudicca and her followers had not even left Hertfordshire when it took place. The battle site was likely to have been somewhere close to Watling Street, as this was surely the route used by both armies. Tacitus tells us that the rebels had large numbers of carts and wagons, filled not only with loot, but also with women and children who had been brought along to witness the anticipated destruction of the Romans. In the event, Boudicca's loose knit, and no doubt ill-disciplined followers were no match for the highly trained and experienced Roman troops, and the wagons, far from providing a grandstand view of the Roman defeat, only served to cut off the line of retreat for the Britons. The Roman victory was complete and Boudicca and her daughters committed suicide; a Roman writer estimated that 80,000 of Boudicca's followers were slaughtered.

THE AFTERMATH OF REVOLT

The effects of the Boudiccan revolt must have been widely felt even where property had not been destroyed. Although it is possible that the only places actually sacked by the rebels lay close to Watling Street, some of the Trinovantes may have used the most direct route, from north Essex by way of Stane Street and Ermine Street, while bands of Iceni could well have swept down the Icknield Way from Norfolk. Certainly these must have been the routes used both by survivors from Boudicca's army as they struggled home and by the avenging Romans who pursued them. Either way, the inhabitants of much of Hertfordshire were now living in what was in effect a war zone. Crops that had not been burnt or looted by the rebels on their outward journey were probably trampled or requisitioned by the Romans in the aftermath. Whatever their persuasion, whether pro- or anti-Roman, the Catuvellauni must have experienced shortages and uncertainty. At Baldock a flock of 98 sheep was slaughtered and cut up for meat at about this time (the bones were found in a pit in 1979). It has been suggested that this resulted from a group of soldiers provisioning themselves in the course of an autumn campaign. Whether these men were Boudicca's followers or soldiers in Paulinus' army we shall never know, but to the owner of the flock the effect must have been equally unfortunate.

It is hardly surprising that one result of the revolt was the construction of military forts. Among local people confidence in the Roman administration must have taken a severe battering, and no doubt Paulinus and his successor established garrisons, not only to restore order in rebel territory, but also to reassure pro-Roman elements in the population. Immediately after the revolt a large fort was built close to the Hertfordshire border at Great Chesterford. This fort covered 35 acres and could have housed up to 4,000 men. At about the same time a smaller fort was established at Little Brickhill, 25 miles along Watling Street to the north-west of Verulamium. Other forts of this date no doubt await discovery and it may well be that some of the finds of Roman military equipment from the county date from the early 60s rather than from the conquest period.

At all events, recovery after the revolt seems to have been rather slow. The fort at Great Chesterford was abandoned in the mid 60s, but it was not until the end of the 70s that town life was really re-established at Verulamium. Similarly, the farmstead at Gorhambury, just outside Verulamium, which had been a thriving concern in the 50s, was reduced by the late 60s to a number of simple round huts.

LOCAL ADMINISTRATION UNDER THE ROMANS

Celtic tribes were normally subdivided into small clans or 'pagi'. A *pagus* was basically a group of people, probably all distantly related to each other, rather than a unit of land, and the extent of the territory controlled by a particular *pagus* must have varied from time to time. By the time of the conquest of AD 43, the *pagi* of Hertfordshire and Essex had coalesced into a larger group, the Catuvellauni, which the Roman authorities described as a *civitas* or state. Since the time of the emperor Augustus (BC30-14AD), the Roman authorities had generally used the *civitas* rather than the *pagus* as the basic unit of administration. In Roman Britain each *civitas* had its own administrative centre, where the tribal council or *ordo* met to decide tribal affairs. The *ordo* was made up of

100 *decuriones* who were recruited from the aristocratic families of the various *pagi* that made up the *civitas*. Each year the *decuriones* chose four of their number to serve as magistrates and administrators (two senior and two junior).

In the Roman period the Catuvellaunian *civitas* was exceptionally large; indeed it was among the largest in Britain. It covered not only Hertfordshire, but Buckinghamshire, Middlesex, Oxfordshire, Northamptonshire and parts of Cambridgeshire. The *civitas* centre was at Verulamium; Baldock and Braughing may also have been centres for *pagi*, but due to the Roman policy of centralising administration, both were now down graded, while encouragement was given to develop Verulamium.

Alongside this Roman form of administration, traditional systems must have continued to function. Caesar tells us that they were based on patrons and clients: a patron was someone of superior wealth and social standing who assisted and protected his clients; the greater the number of clients a patron had, the greater his prestige. In return the client would perform certain services for the patron; in the pre-Roman period this probably included supporting him in war, while under Roman rule it was more likely to involve providing produce, work or rent.

ROMAN ROADS IN HERTFORDSHIRE

Perhaps the most enduring feature of the Roman landscape of Hertfordshire was its road system. Four major roads ran through the county in the Roman period, Watling Street, Ermine Street, Akeman Street and Stane Street. In addition, the ancient route along the Chiltern escarpment, which was followed by the Icknield Way, remained in use throughout the four centuries of Roman rule. Roman administration relied heavily on an efficient communication system and in Hertfordshire the Roman road network was probably established by the middle of the first century AD. How far this network reflected the lines of existing trackways is unknown, although we can safely assume that such tracks existed, linking the main pre-Roman centres like Baldock, Braughing, Welwyn and Verulamium.

Nevertheless, the Roman road network was very different to anything that had gone before and must have been viewed with awe by the native population. In the early Roman period it was particularly important in ensuring supply lines for the army. Watling Street ran from London, through Elstree to Verulamium and Dunstable, ultimately reaching Chester and the military posts in North Wales. Akeman Street also led west, leaving Watling Street at Verulamium to follow the valley of the Bulbourne through the Chilterns towards Alcester, and ultimately Cirencester and the Welsh marches. Another road that must have been of particular importance in the early years of Roman Britain ran north-east from Verulamium through Welwyn to join Ermine Street, a short distance south of Braughing. Ermine Street was the main road from London to York and the northern frontier of the province. In south-east Hertfordshire it followed the west side of the Lea, before crossing the river at Ware. It then led north to Braughing, before veering slightly north-east to cross the north Chilterns near Barkway. Braughing also lay close to the junction of the fourth major road in the county, Stane Street. This led to Colchester and no doubt in part adopted an earlier route, linking these two important pre-Roman centres. Today the A120 still runs on much the same line (for a general view of the Roman roads in the county see the map on page 8).

Major Roman roads like these were carefully and solidly built, and much of the technical expertise must have been provided by military engineers seconded from the legions, although no doubt the back-breaking work of clearance, ditch digging and gravel extraction fell to gangs of local labourers. Roman roads which continued in use over the centuries have lost all trace of their original structure, and only their straight course cutting across the countryside indicates their Roman origin. There are a few cases in the county where the road fell out of use, or its line was altered, and some of these have been excavated, and their structure recorded. A section of Ermine Street was excavated on the south side of Braughing, where changes in the line of the road in the course of the Roman period meant that remains of the first and second century road still survived. This road was built of rammed gravel on a base of clay marl. Near the edge the cobbles were larger, but this may simply be because those from the centre had been weathered away. With a hard, well-cambered surface between 15 and 20 feet wide, it was typical of Roman roads in the county. Rain-water flowed off the camber and drained into road side ditches which were regularly cleaned out and re-cut. Over 100

Fig.12. Roman Ermine Street, near Hertford Heath. A modern bridleway follows the line of the Roman road.

miles of major Roman roads were built in Hertfordshire alone, representing a remarkable engineering enterprise, comparable in relative terms to the development of the motorway network in the 70s and 80s of the present century. Even in modern Hertfordshire many roads, lanes and footpaths follow lines originally set out by Roman military surveyors in the first century AD (figs. 12,13).

In some parts of Roman Britain small forts were established at intervals of about 20 miles (roughly a day's march) along the main roads. This does not seem to have been the pattern in Hertfordshire, where no forts have yet been discovered. This may well be a result of the pro-Roman attitude among the local tribespeople. Small 'posting stations' would have been needed on the main trunk roads to accommodate the *cursus imperium*, the system of despatch riders and officials on which the central government relied to maintain communications with provincial and military authorities. Official inns or hostels were maintained on the main routes to provide them with accommodation and perhaps a change of horses. Some of the small towns in the county, like Braughing, seem to have included inns or rest houses of this sort. Milestones survive on Roman roads elsewhere, but none are recorded from Hertfordshire; given the lack of local stone, wood may have been used instead.

The roads that have been described so far were all major or trunk roads which were supplemented by secondary roads. One linked Verulamium with Silchester (near Reading) and another branched off the Verulamium to Braughing road, and led north-west to Baldock; in later centuries this road regained its importance and became the Great North Road. In the north and west of the county the Icknield Way was metalled and used throughout the Roman period. In addition to this 'formal' road network there was a host of minor roads which served small settlements, industrial sites and villas. As yet these roads, which were probably only lightly metalled, are still far from fully documented or understood, but they must once have been ubiquitous.

Fig.13. Watling Street today running through Redbourn. *(Copyright St Albans Museums).*

Verulamium – Tribal Capital

The Roman town of Verulamium lay on the south bank of the River Ver, approximately half a mile outside the centre of medieval and modern St Albans. Today the area is covered by the village of St Michael's, Verulamium Park and part of the (private) Gorhambury estate. As the only town in the Catuvellaunian territory with the full set of public buildings, forum, basilica, baths and temples, there can be little doubt that throughout the Roman period Verulamium was the tribal centre for the Catuvellauni. The administrators of the Roman Empire saw towns as the main instruments of local government, and as centres of Romanisation. Here the native people of Britain were encouraged to adopt the social and cultural trappings of Roman life.

As we have seen, there was already an important settlement on the site well before the Roman conquest. A large ditched enclosure which is known to lie deep beneath the modern churchyard in the centre of St Michael's village may have surrounded the 'palace' of the pre-Roman ruler, presumably a member of Cunobelin's family. This enclosure probably also formed the administrative, commercial and social centre of the tribe. Close by was a large contingent of smiths, doubtless working under the patronage of the ruling family. The main industrial quarter probably lay on the edge of the flood plain a short distance west of the 'palace'. Here broken clay moulds, used to cast the blanks for gold, silver and bronze coins, have been found, while traces of huts, including part of a large barn-like 'hall', were recorded beneath the modern A4104. The name Verulamium is a Celtic one, meaning the 'settlement over, or by, the marsh.' Swamps and marshes were places especially venerated by the Celts, and the area west of the 'palace' may have been used for religious or ceremonial meetings. At least one deep shaft of the type frequently used by the Celts for depositing offerings and sacrifices was dug here, and several burials have been found. Overlooking the settlement from the crests of the surrounding hills were two cemeteries, while the

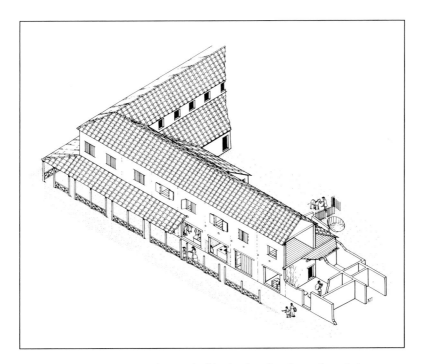

Fig.14. A reconstruction of part of a block of timber framed workshops at Verulamium, which were burnt to the ground during the Boudiccan revolt of AD60. *(Drawn by Alex Thorne).*

whole area was delimited by linear ditches. Beyond these limits lay the farmsteads of prosperous landowners.

After the Roman conquest the pattern of settlement remained very much the same. The ditch of the 'palace' enclosure was allowed to silt up, but a masonry building was put up within it, while to the west, metal working and trading continued to flourish. In about AD 50, someone, presumably a speculator but perhaps the local ruler himself, put up a purpose built block of nine workshops and living quarters, modelled on Roman prototypes (fig. 14). At about the same time a fine *macellum* (market hall) was built facing onto the newly laid out Watling Street, while a Roman bath house was established close to the river. Only a small part of the bath house has been excavated, which is unfortunate because it is currently thought to be the earliest Roman bath house in Britain. It was clearly an impressive structure with a sunken cold plunge bath lined with white

Fig.15. The Forum at Verulamium as it may have appeared in the 3rd century AD. *(From a painting by Alan Sorrell).*

and painted, plastered walls. More than anything else this building speaks of the enthusiasm with which the local ruling family embraced Roman ways.

Whether or not a fort was built at Verulamium at the time of the Roman conquest has long been a matter of argument. Certainly items of Roman military equipment have been recorded from the town. A fine iron *lorica* (body armour) of the type worn by Roman soldiers in the first century was dug from a rubbish pit a short distance outside the Roman town, while small items of horse gear and armour have also been found. Large numbers of lead sling shots, used by the Roman army in catapults, have been found to the south of Verulamium, while the remains of a turf bank on the north edge of the Roman town may have belonged to a Roman fort. The existence of a fort is by no means proved however, and

the bank may simply be part of the early town defences, while the metalwork may be scrap, collected by smiths to refashion into new items.

The first Roman town was burnt to the ground during the Boudiccan revolt, after which it took at least 15 years to recover. So it was only in the last quarter of the first century that the inhabitants became sufficiently prosperous to be able to build the forum and basilica complex which was to be the focus of town life for the next three and a half centuries.

The basilica was an enormous aisled hall, about 400 feet long and 95 feet high. Built in flint, tile and mortar, it would have towered over all other buildings in the town. Its sheer size meant it must have posed tremendous logistical and supply problems to a community totally unused to construction on such a scale. The

Fig.16. An imaginative view of Verulamium from the south as it may have looked in the early 3rd century. *(From a painting by Alan Sorrell)*.

contemporary Roman historian, Tacitus, noted that the British tribes needed substantial government help and encouragement before undertaking this sort of enterprise. The basilica was the legal and administrative centre, where the *decuriones* met, and where the magistrates heard law suits and considered appeals. On its south side was the forum, the town's commercial and religious centre and an open area of about 300 by 200 feet, surrounded by rows of offices and small shops, with at first one and ultimately three classical temples on its south side, probably dedicated to the state gods of Rome (Jupiter, Juno and Minerva) (fig. 15).

The forum and basilica complex at Verulamium was the largest example north of the Alps. It covered the 5-acre site once occupied by the pre-Roman 'palace', and now lies beneath and around St Michael's Church and Vicarage. All that can be seen of it today is one corner of the row of offices on the north-east side of the Basilica, where the flint and mortar foundations have been laid out just outside the Verulamium Museum. Inside the Museum are fragments of the fine marble inscription placed over the entrance to the Basilica on its completion in the autumn of AD 79.

At about the same time that the forum and basilica was being built, the first proper street grid for Verulamium was laid out. The town was divided into square or rectangular blocks (*insulae*) by a grid of metalled streets intersecting one another at right angles. By the end of the first century this grid covered an area of about 100 acres and was partly enclosed by a bank and ditch. Temples were built, some of them probably replacing earlier sacred sites, and work started on a new public bath house. On the west side of the town, the market hall, burnt down in the Boudiccan revolt, was rebuilt, while the block of workshops was also reconstructed on lines very similar to those of its predecessor (fig. 16).

In about AD 140 work started on the construction of a theatre, which today is one of the most noticeable features of the Roman town. It consisted of tiers of wooden seats on a horseshoe shaped bank supported by flint and mortar walls and overlooking a central space, the *orchestra*, beyond which was a raised stage (fig. 17 and front cover). The plan of the Verulamium theatre was

Fig.17. Verulamium theatre today. This aerial photograph shows the large orchestra overlooked by the raised seating banks. In the background, between the theatre and the modern main road, are the foundations of Romano-British shops. *(Copyright St Albans Museums)*.

rather different to that of the 'classical' Graeco-Roman theatre, in that the stage was unusually small and simple, and the *orchestra* unusually large. Indeed, in its earliest version the theatre at Verulamium was something of a compromise between a theatre designed to stage dramatic or comic performances, and an amphitheatre used for games and wild beast shows. It stood directly north of a large temple, occupying a space that seems to have been deliberately set aside for it; certainly it had been kept clear of any buildings from the earliest years of the Roman town. Most archaeologists agree that the theatre had an important religious purpose, perhaps ceremonial games or ritual enactments, as well as more secular activities. Only later on, when the stage was enlarged and embellished and the *orchestra* used for extra seating, do purely dramatic performances seem to have become more important.

Fig. 18. Painted wall plaster from a mid-2nd century house in Verulamium. The mottled wall panels were designed to imitate marble veneers. *(Copyright St Albans Museums).*

Fig. 19. Painted plaster ceiling dating from the late-2nd or early-3rd century, decorated with birds and 'daisy chains'. *(Copyright St Albans Museums).*

The early second century was a prosperous time in Verulamium; industry flourished, and the town steadily expanded. Private houses were built with wood and plaster walls resting on flint and mortar footings, and their interior walls plastered and painted (figs. 18, 19). The remains of several shops and houses of this period have been painstakingly excavated over the last fifty years. Carefully pieced together, the results tell the story not only of the individual buildings, but also of the town and its people. One such house, excavated by Professor Frere in 1959 on the west side of the forum, is a typical example. Here a long, narrow, two roomed shop was built fifteen or twenty years after the Boudiccan revolt. The presence of four small ovens suggests that it may have been owned by a family of bakers, but whatever their trade they

Fig.20. Detail from a well preserved, late 2nd century floor, showing a lion carrying a stag's head. *(Copyright St Albans Museums)*.

prospered sufficiently for the next generation to rebuild the premises to include seven rooms, with painted, plastered walls and mortar floors. The provision of a corridor along one side gave privacy that previously had been lacking; perhaps the household now included slaves or servants. Twenty years later the owners were able to add another wing to their house, and also commissioned a mosaic floor, showing a vase and two leaping dolphins, from a firm of mosaic workers, who operated in both Verulamium and Colchester.

Guests to the house were unable to admire the mosaic for long. No sooner had it been laid out, in about AD 155, than fire swept Verulamium, destroying both the house and a large part of the town. Most buildings were still largely timber framed, and burned easily; nevertheless so intense was the fire that even largely masonry structures like the forum, basilica and baths were completely destroyed.

The task of rebuilding the town must have put a severe strain on local resources, and it was some years before it was complete. The new Verulamium that emerged from the ashes was rather different to its predecessor. The most noticeable difference was that there were now fewer small workshops, and more mansions, some of them with up to twenty rooms on the ground floor alone. Now for the first time houses were built in Verulamium that compared favourably with the comfortable villas of the countryside. Walls and ceilings were painted with sophisticated designs, and many of the 30 mosaic floors known from the town date from this time (figs. 20, 21). Any house with any pretensions had at least one room with under-floor and wall heating provided by a hypocaust; some had their own private bath suites, even though the public baths had been rebuilt after the fire. The mosaic floor and hypocaust of one such bath block is preserved and open to visitors in Verulamium Park.

On their own, the ground plans of the town buildings may appear somewhat lifeless, but it is not difficult to reconstruct the lifestyle of their occupants. Some were obviously the homes of people of modest means. One such house, excavated many years ago by Sir Mortimer Wheeler in the southern part of the town, consisted of a simple two or three roomed house facing onto a main road; for over three centuries the front room was used as a shop and the two small back rooms as living quarters. Most

Fig.21. Mosaic floor with an unusual shell pattern. Late 2nd century. *(Copyright St Albans Museums)*.

houses combined working or business rooms with private domestic accommodation. One enterprising family cashed in on the commercial possibilities presented by the favourable situation of their house between forum, temple and theatre. While the domestic and private rooms were sited away from the street on one side of a partially enclosed courtyard, the street frontage was devoted to a shop and a large public lavatory. Also entered from the street rather than from the 'private' side of the house, was an underground room with a large apsidal alcove at one end, suitable for displaying a small statue. This room was approached directly from the street, by a sloping passage, and it seems, to have been a shrine, possibly dedicated to one of the eastern religions, like the cult of the Egyptian goddess Isis. The shrine seems never to have been finally completed; although the walls were carefully pointed, they were never given their final plaster coat. Perhaps the owner died before work was finished, for the room ended up as an underground cool store. The shrine can still be seen today, close to the A4104.

When it comes to the residences of the town's elite, it is not difficult to see how domestic and business interests were combined under one (large) roof. Several of these wealthy mansions contained a large reception hall, sometimes directly entered from the street. One of these, dating from the very end of the Roman period, was some 40 feet long and contained a magnificent mosaic floor; this was a room that was designed not just to accommodate large numbers of people, but also to impress them. Here the master of the house would receive his tenants and clients, and perhaps collect rent and dues. For private entertaining, any house of any pretension would have an elegant dining room. Here the diners would recline on couches, arranged in three groups of three, on three sides of a central table. These would be placed at one end of the room facing the door so that guests could admire the different courses as they were brought in from the kitchen (fig. 22). Also displayed for the admiration of the guests would be the family silverware, and dining rooms can sometimes be identified

Fig.22. A mosaic floor, discovered in 1932 by Sir Mortimer Wheeler, with an intact hypocaust beneath it. The mouth of the hypocaust is visible at the base of the picture. Hot air from the furnace in the foreground was drawn beneath the floor, and up the walls through hollow flues. *(Copyright St Albans Museums).*

Fig.23. Bronze model of a dinner party guest reclining on a couch. It is possible that this tiny object, found in a rubbish tip just outside Verulamium, was a child's toy. *(Copyright St Albans Museums).*

by the presence of a mosaic floor panel, placed off centre to the room, so that it could easily be seen, rather than being obscured by table and couches (fig. 23). Many of the larger houses were built on two or three sides of open areas, which were probably occupied by formal gardens; these generally face south-east to take full advantage of the sun, and some were overlooked by small projecting annexes which were probably dining rooms.

Outside the town lay extensive cemeteries. Roman law forbade the burial of anyone within a town, with the exception of infants less than 40 days old. The offerings placed in the graves show that many of the townspeople were prosperous, as well as telling us a lot about the people themselves, such as their health, their diet and their life expectancy. Gold plated beads, expertly carved gemstones from finger rings, fine glass and tableware traded from all over the Roman empire, complement the impression of good living provided by the growing number of frescoes and mosaics from the town's houses (figs. 24, 25).

There can be no doubt that late Roman Verulamium's citizens included some of real wealth and culture. A remarkable account is preserved in the medieval records of St Albans Abbey describing how monks in the early eleventh century, digging for building material on the site of the Roman town, uncovered a 'palace' containing book rolls written in Latin and (apparently) Celtic.

Fig.24. Glass vessels from Verulamium. *(Copyright St Albans Museums)*.

Fig.25. A ceramic beaker, decorated with a lively hunting scene in which a hound chases a hare. It demonstrates how the Celtic love of curvilinear decoration persisted through the Roman period. *(Copyright St Albans Museums)*.

These books seem to have included lists of religious festivals, so it is possible that they were part of the official records kept in the basilica, but the possibility remains that they came from a private library. Needless to say none survived the zeal of the medieval monks, who saw them as the works of the devil, and burned them.

In spite of this increased emphasis on gracious living Verulamium retained its industrial and commercial roles. Many of the large town houses had ranges of rather box-like, functional rooms. These may well have been workrooms used by craftsmen who previously had worked in separate workshops, but who were now accommodated in service wings in their patron's mansion.

Perhaps the best way to reconstruct a picture of everyday life in Roman Verulamium is to try to see it through the eyes of an imaginary visitor in, for instance, the early third century. By this time it had more or less recovered from the effects of the fire of 155, and was a busy market town. The main approach roads were lined with wooden workshops, tanneries, smithies, stockyards and cemeteries. No doubt a pall of smoke often hung across the valley, and when the wind was in the north-west the stench of the tanneries outside the town must have been overwhelming. Attempts were sometimes made to keep the more unpleasant industrial processes away from town centres, but as with the maintenance of the streets and water supply, much depended on the energy and efficiency of the town magistrates. Reaching the centre, the visitor would have been confronted by a collection of truly splendid public buildings. Today all that remains are at best isolated foundations, or more often just the trenches where medieval builders dug out the Roman stone. In Verulamium's heyday however the temples, baths, and forum were all probably decorated with statues, carvings, and inscriptions, as well as tessellated floors, tiled roofs and marble veneers, and would have compared favourably with anything other tribal capitals in Britain could afford. Overlooking the town centre from the hill on the other side of the river was the temple on the site of the royal burial at Folly Lane. By the early third century this was already probably one of the oldest buildings in the town, but the edge of the sacred precinct had recently been marked out by a broad band of gleaming white chalk, clearly visible from the town below.

In the town centre the street frontages were closely built up, with shops and workshops jostling each other for space. Some shops were simply the 'fronts' of larger establishments, opening on to yards and with the main residential quarters sited a bit away from the noise of the street. One of these 'courtyard' houses was probably a *mansio* or official guest house, where our hypothetical visitor might well have been put up. Any visitor to the town would probably make use of the public baths, which were its main social centre, and he might drop in on the small cook shop with brewery attached which prospered for three hundred years on the street corner opposite. On market days ox-carts trundled into Verulamium from the surrounding countryside, bringing local farmers and peasants with their surplus produce to sell or barter in the forum. No doubt there were also seasonal festivals, such as cattle and horse fairs, and these together with religious festivals would have drawn in still larger crowds. So great were the numbers attracted to the temples by the theatre and the royal burial site that a special relief road seems to have been built to accommodate them.

THE DEFENCES OF VERULAMIUM

Verulamium was given a bank and ditch defence shortly after the Boudiccan revolt, perhaps in a belated attempt to assure local people that the Roman state would protect them. In the course of the early second century these defences gradually silted up and in time were built over. Shortly before the fire of 155 a start was made on a new bank and ditch which more or less doubled the size of the enclosed area. The precise line of this defence, known as the Fosse, is still unclear and it is not even certain that the earthwork was ever completed; some scholars think that work on it was abandoned after the fire. On the other hand, excavations on the Fosse in the 1930s showed that in several places the ditch had been re-cut, and the bank heightened. This suggests that the Fosse was not only completed, but that it was in use long enough to require a certain amount of refurbishment. There is no obvious reason why it was thought necessary to defend Verulamium in the mid second century, but it is possible that the refurbishment (if that it what it was) took place at the end of the century at a time when several other towns in Roman Britain were being given earthwork defences. Some archaeologists see the late second century town defences as a reflection of the political uncertainties that affected

Fig.26. The walls of Roman Verulamium. *(Copyright St Albans Museums).*

Fig.27. A model of the south-east gate of Verulamium as it may have looked in the 3rd century. *(Copyright St Albans Museums).*

the empire at this time, and it has been suggested that the reason why some villas in the Verulamium district seem to have fallen on hard times at the start of the third century was due to the land-owning class backing the losing political faction.

In the course of the third century however Verulamium's authorities embarked on an even more ambitious project, the construction of the town walls. This was a major enterprise at least as demanding as the original construction of the forum and basilica. The River Ver was canalised, and the marsh to the north of the town drained. This meant that the wall could be extended along the north side of the town, so that in all it ran for over 2 miles and enclosed an area of over 203 acres, making Verulamium the third largest town in Roman Britain, after London and Cirencester (fig. 26).

Unfortunately the Roman wall provided a particularly con-venient source of building material for the medieval Abbey of St Alban, and all that remains today is the core, a mixture of flint nodules and mortar bonded together with regular courses of tile. In many places only the foundations survive. Originally how-ever the wall was probably 13 feet high, carefully faced with dressed flints, with four imposing gateways surmounted by towers (fig. 27). The length of the walls however was far too great to be effectively manned if attacked, and their main purpose seems to have been to provide Verulamium with an imposing and pres-tigious appearance – as a monument to the civic pride and wealth of its third century citizens.

Although Verulamium continued as a prosperous market town the troubles of the Roman empire as a whole were bound to affect it sooner or later. The last years of the Roman town will be looked at in more detail in the last chapter; all that needs saying here is that with the final departure of the Roman army from Britain in the early fifth century trade and industry gradually dwindled. Gradually the population declined as people drifted away, either to the countryside or to the Christian settlement that was estab-lishing itself around St Alban's shrine on the opposite side of the river.

Baldock and Braughing

Baldock lies on the chalk escarpment at a point where the Icknield Way crosses a natural route through the Chilterns by way of the Hitchin gap. This combination of a natural route centre with easily worked farmland made it an ideal position for early settlement, and it is hardly surprising that there was a thriving community here well before the Roman conquest. As is usual with such settlements in Hertfordshire, early Baldock was a sprawling collection of farmsteads, stockyards, enclosures and trackways with a sprinkling of cemeteries, isolated burials and industrial areas. The whole complex covered an area of about 5,000 acres. The earliest evidence for settlement so far discovered comes from burials; one cemetery in particular included several rich graves dating from between the early first century BC and the mid-1st century AD. One of the earliest contained a bronze cauldron, an Italian wine jar (*amphora*), two bronze dishes, two iron firedogs, two bronze mounted buckets, and a pig's skeleton. The dead man himself had apparently been cremated wrapped in a bear's skin; and since it is unlikely that bears were roaming Hertfordshire in the first century BC, this too was presumably a luxury import. Another early burial lay within a large ditched enclosure and included part of an iron mail shirt. The surrounding ditch contained two human skeletons and the whole complex is similar in many ways to the royal burial site at Folly Lane, outside Verulamium, though smaller and less elaborate. These magnificent collections of grave offerings give us a vivid picture of the life style of the local warlords turned middlemen who exploited the trading opportunities provided by the Roman Empire as it expanded into Gaul.

As elsewhere in the county, the Roman conquest does not seem to have led to military occupation in Baldock. There is no sign of a Roman fort, and apart from possible troubles during or after the Boudiccan revolt, this peaceful state of affairs seems to have lasted throughout the Roman period. Several trackways that had been first laid out in the pre-Roman period were extended and metalled in the later part of the first century AD, and were then used right through to the fourth century. Just as at Verulamium, Baldock developed on lines laid down well before the coming of Rome.

In spite of the undoubted prosperity of its leading families in the pre-Roman period, under Roman rule Baldock seems to have been a fairly modest market town. This was no doubt partly due to the road network. Although the Icknield Way continued to be used throughout the Roman period and beyond, the main Roman road to the north, Ermine Street, ran further east, and Baldock's only other means of communication was by secondary roads connecting it with Braughing and Verulamium to the south and the minor Roman settlement at Sandy (in Bedfordshire) to the north.

Modern excavations are almost invariably carried out on sites which are about to be destroyed by redevelopment, which in Baldock's case has by chance led to the excavation of few houses and a large number of Roman cemeteries, from which nearly 2,000 Romano-British graves have been excavated. As is normal on Romano-British settlement sites, Baldock's cemeteries were placed on the outskirts of the built-up areas. They ring approximately 43 acres between Clothall Road and the High Street, presumably circling the heart of the Roman town.

East of the modern Clothall Road, the system of trackways, farmsteads and enclosures that was established in the pre-Roman Iron Age continued throughout much of the Roman period. Early in the third century AD one enclosure was provided with an elaborate timber gateway, but inside it circular wooden houses of the type commoner in the Iron Age were still being built. Rectangular buildings certainly existed however, and there is evidence suggesting that some at least of these were provided with substantial flint and mortar foundations and may once have been quite imposing. Several wells are known, while corn-processing ovens suggest that, not surprisingly, agriculture was the main means of support for the townspeople. An iron smelting furnace, a number of crucibles and several half completed bronze brooches show that metalworking was also carried out. No doubt Baldock functioned as a local market centre where surplus produce could be sold, and where specialised items (like brooches) which could not be produced on rural farmsteads were made and either sold or bartered.

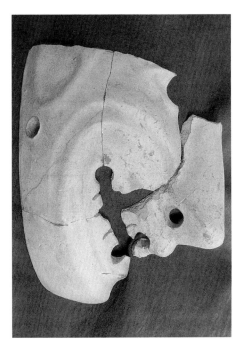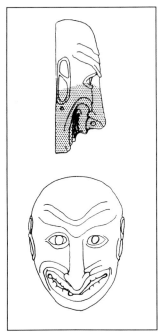

Fig.28. Fragment from a ceramic theatrical mask from Baldock. The line drawing (after Stead and Rigby) shows the mask as it would have been when complete; the shading indicates the existing portion. *(Copyright North Herts District Council Museums Service)*.

For much of the Roman period Baldock had an important additional function, that of a local religious centre. It has already been suggested that in the pre-Roman period it was the base for an extremely wealthy family, and it is not unlikely that it was the centre for a sub-group or *pagus* of the Catuvellauni. Such a centre might well have maintained its own religious cult, and certainly in comparison to other Roman remains, Baldock has produced a disproportionate amount of religious or ritual finds. The foundations of a Romano-Celtic temple have been discovered from the air, but not, as yet, excavated. More unusual is the fragment of a theatrical mask found near the centre of modern Baldock (fig. 28). This shows a well modelled but grotesque, ceramic mask, similar to the theatrical masks used by comic actors in Roman theatres. The Baldock example however is too large and heavy actually to have been used as a mask, and as it is rather unlikely that the town had a theatre in which classical drama was performed it has been suggested that the mask was part of the decoration of a public building, possibly a temple. More remarkable still was the discovery of a model spear, two model axes, and 44 iron spears, most of which were found in a single pit, dating from the third century. All these objects seem to be votive offerings to a god. Who this god was we do not yet know. One possibility is Silvanus, god of woodlands and hunting, another is a horse-riding warrior god, to whom the Catuvellauni seem to have been particularly devoted.

The final years of Roman Baldock are obscure. Situated on the Icknield Way it must have been vulnerable to any attackers coming along the ridgeway from East Anglia or the Thames valley. Nevertheless there is no sign of any sudden or catastrophic end to the settlement; rather there seems to have been a gradual process of desertion and decay. The Roman cemeteries, dating from the late fourth century, are nearer to the core settlement area, suggesting that by now this core was shrinking in size. Later still, on the farmsteads and enclosures on the eastern outskirts of the town, the bones of deer, foxes and hares have been found in the mouths of wells and pits, suggesting that the wells were no longer maintained, and wild animals were roaming across once cultivated fields.

BRAUGHING

Today Braughing is a pleasant village, but in the last quarter of the first century BC it was the most important trading settlement in southern England, where more luxury goods brought in from the Continent have been found than anywhere else. The rise in importance of Verulamium in the early first century AD led to the relative decline of Braughing. Nevertheless the settlement's prosperity lasted well into the Roman period. Braughing had started life as a trading post, conveniently situated at a natural route centre. In the Roman period this favourable position was exploited as existing trackways were brought into the provincial road network. Ermine Street, connecting London and Lincoln, passed through Braughing, while Stane Street, *en route* for Colchester, ran a short distance to the south. Minor roads also led to the south Midlands via Baldock, and north-east to Great Chesterford. The River Rib may well have been navigable for flat bottomed boats, and 7 miles south of Braughing it fed into the Lea which was certainly navigable.

In about AD 80 Braughing was provided with a network of

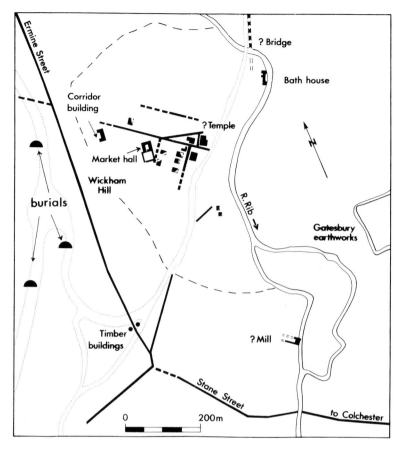

Fig.29. A plan of Roman Braughing. The Roman streets are shown as heavy black lines, the modern roads as dotted lines. Compare this plan with the air photograph of the same area, fig 30. *(Drawn by Alex Thorne, after Clive Partridge).*

streets, replacing the lightly metalled tracks of the earlier settlement. The full Roman street pattern in Braughing is by no means understood yet, but it looks as if a regular street grid was planned in the later first century, similar to that which was being laid out at Verulamium at much the same time. The late first century also saw its first masonry buildings. A substantial Roman bath house was built on the east end of Wickham Hill. This was rather small for a public bath, although it had an impressive number of rooms and was solidly built with flint and plastered and painted mortar walls and mortared floors. It is possible that the baths were associated with a *mansio*, an official guest house used by couriers on government business. On the other hand, Braughing may have been a *pagus* centre, and the bath house part of the residence of the official responsible for local administration. Nearby was a large L-shaped building, built with dressed limestone blocks, whose purpose is unknown, but may have been a *macellum* (market hall) or a temple. Remains of at least four other masonry buildings are known, although so far none has been fully excavated. Aerial photography has located a house, similar in plan to some villas, with rooms opening off a connecting corridor, and with projecting wings at either end. Less is known about the other buildings, but their very existence argues for a level of Romanisation not seen elsewhere in Hertfordshire away from Verulamium and the large villas.

Alongside these relatively pretentious buildings were small workshops strung out along the main street. These were built on the normal Romano-British plan with a larger room, possibly fronted by a verandah, opening onto the street and smaller compartments behind serving as the living quarters. Debris from bone-working and metal-working indicate some of the trades practised here, but other craftsmen no doubt settled here too.

As in so many Romano-British settlements, there is clear evidence that religion played a central role in the life of the community. In the pre-Roman period the area between Station Road and Wickham Park may have been an important sacred site. Here a rectilinear ditched enclosure was excavated in the early 1980s. The ditch contained remains of seventeen human skeletons as well as quantities of animal bone, and it is possible that these are the remains of sacrificial offerings at a Celtic shrine. It has been suggested that the L-shaped building on Wickham Hill may have been a Roman temple, and finds of figurines and a lead curse are just the sort of objects associated with Romano-British temples. Lead curses were plaques of lead on which were scratched requests to the god to punish a thief (or sometimes a rival in love) who had made off with someone else's property; the request was usually accompanied by a promise to reward the god with a suitable offering if the stolen property was recovered. The curse was then nailed up in the temple for everyone to see. Unfortunately the Braughing curse is now totally indecipherable, so we shall never know what it was that the unfortunate Braughing resident had

Fig.30. Air photograph of the centre of Braughing. The main street leading from the river towards Ermine Street can be seen as a pale strip. Side roads branching off it are also visible. Two narrow white lines at the right hand end of the main street may mark the foundations of a temple. *(Copyright Cambridge University Collection of Air Photographs)*.

lost, or what revenge he thought it justified.

Sadly Romano-British Braughing does not seem to have lived up to its promising start. The bath house fell into disuse in the second century and was gradually demolished. No defences were ever built and the offerings in graves excavated on the edge of the settlement all suggest a modest affluence, but no great flowering of wealth to match the trading boom of the first century BC. For most of the Roman period Braughing seem to have been a small road-side town, servicing the needs of the surrounding district and profiting from passing trade along Ermine Street. Its history seems to have been peaceful, not to say uneventful; there is no sign in the archaeological record of the Boudiccan revolt, of the troubles of the later Roman empire, or of the coming of the Saxons. This being said however, we must always bear in mind that the apparent absence of many substantial buildings may simply reflect the absence of excavation in the core of the town. One of the fascinations of archaeology is that it could take only one or two excavations in the centre of the Roman settlement to radically alter this view.

Minor Towns

The main problem in dealing with the smaller Roman towns in Hertfordshire is one of terminology. When do we classify a settlement as a small town rather than a rural settlement? The problem is really one of scale. The largest town in Roman Hertfordshire was Verulamium, which, even at its period of greatest prosperity, may only have had a population of between 5,000 and 10,000. Lesser towns like Baldock and Braughing probably only had half this number, and so in today's terms would be small villages. Further down the scale the Roman settlements at Cow Roast, Ware and Welwyn were smaller still.

COW ROAST

The Roman name of the settlement at Cow Roast has been long forgotten, and today it is named after the public house on the old A41 between Berkhamsted and Tring, which lies more or less in the centre of the Roman settlement. Before the Roman conquest this area had been an important iron producing centre using the iron ore that occurs naturally in the glacial clay on the slopes around the Ashridge estate and Berkhamsted Common. After the conquest there may have been a Roman fort here. Many years ago a Roman helmet was found on the edge of the iron working area, at Northchurch, while the large number of coins of the emperor Claudius that have been found on the site may reflect the presence of soldiers with money to spend. The settlement flourished throughout the second and third centuries, spreading along both sides of Akeman Street. Aerial photographs have revealed side lanes leading off the main road, dividing the area up into blocks. The buildings themselves have left little or no trace, and they are likely to have been modest timber workshops, similar to countless other examples from Roman Britain. Chance finds of pottery, coins and small items of metalwork from the settlement suggest living standards comparable to those on small farming communities like Foxholes Farm (described in the next chapter).

Nevertheless there were clearly well-to-do families in the area. Remains of substantial buildings with solid, flint and mortar walls have been recorded in Berkhamsted and Rails Copse, while at Northchurch a comfortable villa has been excavated. There is evidence for a second villa close by, while at Dudswell there are records of a hypocaust, perhaps indicating a third villa. Not all of these buildings were necessarily occupied at the same time but they certainly indicate prosperity, at least for a section of the population. Nevertheless the status of the Roman settlement as a whole is still uncertain. Was it a small town occupied by iron smelters who supplemented their livelihood by servicing travellers along Akeman Street, with successful ironworkers building themselves comfortable residences on the outskirts, or does it represent the quarters of estate workers, who spent their lives toiling in the service of affluent patrons or landlords? In the present state of knowledge all we can say is that for most of the Roman period this stretch of what is now the A4251 ran through a thickly populated industrial area which was overlooked by two or three prosperous villas, set well away from the noise and smoke of the iron works.

By the fourth century activity at Cow Roast seems to have been declining. Iron working relied on large quantities of charcoal to fuel the furnaces and it may be that centuries of charcoal burning had led to serious deforestation, and a consequent decline in the industry on which the settlement depended.

WARE

Excavations in the 1970s showed that at the time of the Roman conquest there was a thriving settlement on the north side of the Lea. Substantial amounts of pottery as well as sizeable ditches suggest that Ware then enjoyed considerable economic importance.

The Roman settlement also grew up on the north bank of the Lea, slightly to the west of the modern town centre, near the point at which Ermine Street crossed the river. Excavations near the site of the Glaxo factory on the west side of the town have recovered a few bronze fittings of the sort used by the Roman army to secure leather straps and belts. It is possible that shortly after the conquest a detachment of Roman soldiers was stationed here, perhaps working on road and bridge building. By the second century Ware was a busy industrial and road side settlement. Pottery kilns, bone working, grain processing and metalworking have all left their traces but remains of the Roman buildings themselves are confined to faint traces of wattle and daub or timber framed buildings flanking Ermine Street. Associated with them were numerous ovens and furnaces.

One building may have been a wayside shrine, and two small 'triple vases', possibly used to burn incense and now in the Ware museum, were found on the site. Most of the buildings seem to have been 'work-a-day' smithies and workshops. Nevertheless a late Roman burial in an expensive lead coffin from the Glaxo site indicates a certain amount of wealth in the community, and it may be that there were more affluent areas in the settlement that have not yet been discovered. Certainly by the late Roman period, Ware lay at the heart of one of the more economically prosperous parts of Hertfordshire. Not only was the settlement on an important road on a navigable river, but it was close to the thriving pottery industry at Hadham, and the products of the potteries were almost certainly shipped down the Lea from Ware.

Among the more unusual discoveries to have been made in Ware are an iron slave chain, and a late Roman well, lined with wooden boards, some of which were still preserved in the water-logged subsoil. The well contained the complete skeletons of several pigs and dogs, but how these came to be down a well is another mystery we shall never resolve.

WELWYN

It has become clear in recent years that in both the Roman, and pre-Roman periods, there were several settlements in and around what today is the village of Welwyn on the banks of the River Mimram, and in Welwyn Garden City, approximately three miles to the south-east. Indeed, at the time of the Roman conquest homesteads, fields, enclosures, industrial areas and cemeteries were spread over much of the area between the rivers Mimram and Lea. The gradual discovery of the area's significance has been almost entirely due to the efforts of the local society of amateur archaeologists, led by Tony Rook. What is more, this thriving community included a particularly rich and influential group of people. Three rich burials, dating from the century before the Roman conquest, have been discovered in the area, and are among the richest of their date from the country. In these graves, the so called Welwyn chieftains' burials, the cremated ashes of the dead were accompanied by exceptionally rich grave offerings, including exotic luxury goods imported from the Mediterranean world.

What happened in Welwyn after the conquest is less certain, but gradually occupation seems to have become focused near the centre of present day Welwyn village, around the point at which the Roman road from Verulamium to Braughing and Colchester crossed the Mimram. This major road, together with a lesser road leading north-east to Baldock, provided local people with a convenient trading outlet as well as the opportunity of selling goods and services direct to passing travellers and officials.

Two villas have been excavated on the eastern side of Welwyn; the first was discovered many years ago at Lockleys and the other more recently at Dicket Mead. Further masonry remains are known to lie close to the centre of the modern village half a mile up stream from the villa sites, and Welwyn archaeologists have recorded traces of Roman occupation over a wide area. It seems certain that the Roman settlement covered at least 100 acres and no doubt further 'high status' sites await discovery, as well as the more modest establishments occupied by agricultural and industrial workers. Further afield traces of Romano-British occupation have been recorded north-east of Welwyn itself, as well as on the south and east towards Stanborough and Welwyn Garden City.

By and large the local Romano-British inhabitants were probably the descendants of the original pre-Roman population. The local aristocratic family or families hinted at by the 'chieftain' graves, probably succeeded in maintaining their position under Roman rule. Certainly there were affluent people living in the area, who by the third century had acquired distinctly civilised tastes. Some of the most intriguing finds from the county have been published recently by Tony Rook, and include fragments of expertly carved sculptures in Greek marble. An elaborate mausoleum near Welwyn Hall produced part of a Greek marble sarcophagus while fragments of a marble statue (possibly of the god Apollo) and a sculpture relief of a horse or stag were found on the site of the Dicket Mead villa. All three sculptures were expertly carved by a master craftsman, and it has been suggested that they are the work of a Greek sculptor working in the area for sophisticated local patrons. This suggestion is supported by the discovery, again at Dicket Mead, of a small amulet made of haematite. This was a magic charm, designed to protect women in childbirth, and was engraved with a mixture of Judaic and Greek inscriptions along with a representation of the Egyptian goddess Isis. This remarkable little object surely suggests the presence in Welwyn of immigrants from the Mediterranean; it is not too far fetched to see them as a group of Greek sculptors and their womenfolk.

The basis of wealth in this part of Roman Hertfordshire must have been the production of grain. Large numbers of corn drying ovens have been recorded from the Welwyn area, suggesting that grain processing was carried on a commercial scale, particularly in the later Roman period. Pottery production was also carried out, continuing an industry that started here much earlier.

In spite of the great increase in the amount of information that has been collected recently, it is still rather difficult to say whether Roman Welwyn was a small town, or a number of wealthy villa estates, with workers' settlements nearby. Numerous Roman burials have been excavated, particularly in an extensive cemetery with some 4,000 graves close to the modern civic centre in Welwyn village, but whether the people buried here were drawn from an extensive rural area or whether they were the inhabitants of a small town, remains a question that only further excavation will resolve. In many ways however, Welwyn resembles Cow Roast, with agriculture and small scale luxury enterprises like sculpture taking the place of the metalworking industry at Cow Roast.

The Countryside and Farming

Throughout the Roman period the vast majority of the population were country people. For many, visits to the towns would have been rare occurrences, perhaps confined to religious festivals, occasional markets, or the periodic census when taxes were assessed.

At the time of the Roman conquest most ordinary people passed their lives in small agricultural communities or scattered farmsteads. This pattern of life was too well established to be quickly changed with the advent of Roman rule. It has been estimated that in north-east Hertfordshire roughly 80% of the Romano-British rural settlements are on sites that were already occupied in the century before the arrival of the Roman army. Figures like this suggest that so far as the countryside was concerned, the Roman conquest brought little disruption; indeed for many rural communities life was largely unchanged for several generations.

Unfortunately, like their late Iron Age predecessors, the remains of Romano-British peasant settlements are both fragile and inconspicuous; they are not easily recognised but are all too easily destroyed by ploughing, quarrying or building. Even in areas where these settlements are known or suspected, few have so far been excavated. Of one thing we can be sure, and that is that the number of rural settlements shown on the map of Roman Hertfordshire is merely the tip of the iceberg, and represents only a fraction of those that originally existed. Over the centuries the remains of dozens of hamlets, farmsteads and small settlements must have been totally destroyed (figs.31, 32).

In the early Roman period the buildings themselves were invariably timber framed, sometimes resting on sleeper beams laid on the surface of the ground or in shallow slots, sometimes supported by wooden posts, their bases dug into the ground and 'firmed in' with a clay or flint packing. The walls themselves may occasionally have been boards or logs (a fine boarded warehouse

Fig.31. Excavating a rural site in north Hertfordshire. *(Copyright North Herts Museums Service)*.

Fig.32. Air photograph of a ditched enclosure near Sandridge. Small ditched enclosures, are typical of Romano-British and pre-Roman sites in Hertfordshire. *(Copyright St Albans Museums)*.

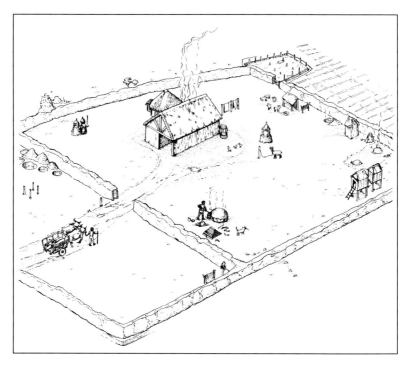

Fig.33. Imaginative reconstruction of a farmstead based on excavated sites like that at Foxholes Farm. A thatched, wooden farmhouse stands in a hedged enclosure, with a round house close by. Raised granaries, hay drying racks, privies, rubbish pits and a small metalworking hearth are also shown. On the top right of the drawing is a small cemetery. *(Drawn by Alex Thorne)*.

dating from the later first century AD was excavated recently in London), but they were usually made of lath and clay. In the first century the roofs were either thatched or shingled, but as time went on clay roof tiles were frequently used. Inside the floors were either of beaten clay, chalk, cobbles or planks, although a few made of flint are known. Because the remains of houses of this sort are particularly vulnerable to the effects of ploughing and erosion, few complete building plans have survived.

One such homestead was excavated in the late 1970s by Clive Partridge. The site lay at Foxholes Farm, a mile south-east of Hertford. The site was first occupied centuries before the Roman conquest, and by the middle of the first century AD a rectangular enclosure had been laid out, covering 2.5 acres and surrounded by a bank and ditch. In the Roman period a rectangular wooden building was erected and the ditch was allowed to silt up. Fields, droveways and enclosures spread across the surrounding area, and mixed farming formed the basis of the settlement's prosperity. By the third and fourth centuries arable farming was more important, and remains of five corn-drying ovens have survived, at least one of which seems to have been used to malt barley for brewing beer (fig. 33). Experiments carried out on a replica of one Foxholes Farm oven showed that it would have been of little use for simply drying large quantities of grain, but that it was far more efficient if used to warm barley as the first step in the beer brewing process. From its earliest years the Romano British inhabitants of Foxholes Farm built small blacksmithing hearths, and smithing seems to have become increasingly important as time went on; altogether 40 metalworking hearths were excavated on the site.

Similar sites are known right across the county. In the extreme north-west, at Pirton at the foot of the Chiltern escarpment, part of a Romano-British hamlet was excavated in 1989. Pirton seems to have been continuously occupied by a small farming community from the first century BC until the sixth or seventh century AD. Like Foxholes Farm it started life as a fairly modest settlement, but as time went on, the inhabitants prospered and pottery imported from the Continent and other 'luxury' goods made their appearance on the site. The second and centuries AD seem to have been its time of greatest prosperity, when some of the houses were provided with flint and mortar foundations and plastered walls. Iron was worked on the site and chalk pits were dug nearby. For most of its life however Pirton consisted of a varying number of small timber buildings surrounded by tracks, storage pits, field ditches and droveways.

Another example of this sort of peasant settlement is known on the outskirts of Amersham, just over the Hertfordshire/ Buckinghamshire border at Mantles Green. Here occupation probably started towards the end of the first century AD and by the middle of the next century a small scale but thriving iron-working concern was operating, cheek by jowl with cattle pens and stockyards. A century later the iron working enterprise had been given up and a small rectangular house with flint and mortar foundations was surrounded by yard surfaces and small ditches. Later still, in the fourth century, two corn-drying ovens were built; when excavated one of them still contained burnt grains of wheat

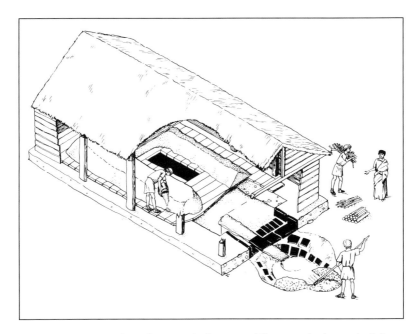

Fig.34. Reconstruction of a corn-drying oven. These worked on principles similar to those of hypocausts. Corn was heaped on a raised floor, under which hot air from a furnace circulated through central and side flues. *(Drawn by Alex Thorne)*.

and oats. These, together with fragments of querns, again underline the importance of arable farming at this date, while numerous animal bones and traces of droveways and palisaded stock enclosures indicate a thriving mixed farm economy (fig. 34).

Evidence of Romano-British occupation of a similarly unpretentious character has been recorded over many years in the Bishops Stortford area. At Thorley, to the south of the modern village, remains of small rectangular timber buildings with mortar floors have been recorded. These seem to date from the fourth century AD, but the presence of earlier Roman pottery suggests that occupation started well before this. The settlement seems to have extended over a considerable area as remains of third century wooden buildings have been recorded north of Stane Street, while Roman pottery and burials have been recorded on several sites in Bishops Stortford.

Although only four peasant settlements have been described in any detail here, many more are known, and even more must still await discovery. These are the settlements that formed the basis of

Roman Hertfordshire. Today their remains may look uninspiring, but originally they were probably no worse than many of the cottages inhabited by the rural poor until comparatively recently. Nor does the fact that many Romano-British farmers in Hertfordshire chose to build their homes in the traditional styles of their ancestors, rather than in the alien style of Rome, necessarily mean that they were poverty-stricken. We have only to look at the wine and olive oil jars from France, Italy and Spain, that are frequently found on these sites, or at the serviceable knives and tools, the enamelled brooches, the spoons, pins, figurines and lamps, to realise that the families that lived here were some way removed from mere subsistence levels.

At the end of a hard, and by our standards rather short life, the inhabitants of these small hamlets were laid to rest in small cemeteries on the outskirts of the settlement. Sometimes the only surviving trace of these little communities is a small group of cremations or inhumation burials buried just beneath the reach of modern ploughs.

FARMING IN ROMAN HERTFORDSHIRE

Since the 1970s a great deal of new information on agriculture in Roman Hertfordshire has come to light. This has largely been due to the development of new techniques enabling significant quantities of preserved seeds and other plant remains to be gathered relatively quickly and simply. Meanwhile the study of animal bones from excavations has become more detailed, and a series of aerial surveys has provided much new information on the settlements themselves.

Most of the rural sites known from Roman Hertfordshire are surrounded by areas of land on which weathered fragments of pottery, tile and other domestic debris are found scattered across the modern fields. These remains may spread over quite wide areas, and are thought to derive from Romano-British household rubbish heaps and middens which were carted out and used to manure the surrounding fields. If correct, this implies that even the smallest rural settlement in Roman Hertfordshire was surrounded by arable fields, fertilised by household rubbish and farmyard waste. In areas with heavy clay soils marling was also carried out, adding lime to the soil.

In recent years a number of Roman field systems have been recognised in the county. Some fields are defined by low banks, which were gradually built up as weeds and stones were piled on the edges, while in the Chilterns ploughed soil was washed down a sloping field to pile up against its lower edge and form lynchets. Examples of lynchets can still been seen in the Chess valley north-west of Latimer, and along the Chiltern escarpment at Pirton. Other fields were enclosed by shallow ditches, which today are only visible from the air. Generally the Romano-British fields were square or rectangular, usually between 2 and 5 acres in extent. Traces of them have been recorded on the outskirts of Verulamium, and at Radwell in the north of the county.

On some rural sites other agricultural features have been recognised. A large barn, associated with ditches which may mark the line of droveways and stockpens, has been recorded just outside Verulamium. Whether the barn was used to store farm produce or to house farm workers is still uncertain; it may have been used by both workers and livestock living together in a 'hall' house. Such buildings have been recorded elsewhere in Roman Britain, but like so much else their precise function is not known.

The tools that the Romano-British farmer had at his disposal were not all that dissimilar to those of his Iron Age predecessors. One of the most important in the heavy soils of Hertfordshire must have been the ploughshare. At the beginning of the Roman period this was just a primitive *ard*; a wooden beam with an iron tip or sheath, which could cut the soil but not turn it over. Several of these simple shares are known from the county. The technique used by Romano-British farmers seems to have been to plough the fields in one direction, and then to turn and plough it again at right angles, forming a chequer effect of plough furrows, the bases of which are occasionally found in excavations. There is evidence suggesting that later in the Roman period ploughs with wooden mould boards, capable of turning the soil over as well as cutting through it, were introduced.

As well as ploughs, wooden spades and shovels were used. The iron tips of these are all that survive today. Other tools included iron pruning hooks, hoes, sickles and scythes (these last were probably used for cutting hay).

In the Iron Age and Roman period, grain that was not going to be used as seed corn was sometimes heated and dried so as to prevent it sprouting in the damp, mild winters, and to make it easier to thresh. Specialised ovens were built for this purpose – the so called corn-drying ovens – which became especially common in the late Roman period. Corn-drying ovens were also used for malting grain. Beer was a popular drink in Roman Britain and many of the Hertfordshire ovens would have been used for malting. Even in these specialised ovens mistakes were sometimes made and grain was accidentally burnt. From the archaeologists' point of view this is a blessing, since heavily charred grains survive which in the normal course of events would have long since disappeared. Finds of charred grain suggest that wheat was the most important arable crop in Roman Hertfordshire, followed by barley. Occasionally grains of rye are found, but it is uncertain whether rye was grown intentionally, or whether the grains are simply those of weeds growing in the crop.

By the middle of the Iron Age the primitive grinding stones used by earlier generations to grind corn were being replaced by more efficient rotary querns, and these became ubiquitous in the Roman period. By the fourth century a wealthy farmer with the labour and resources at his disposal might commission a water mill on his land. In 1992 what are thought to be the remains of a water

Fig.35. Corn-drying oven or malting oven from Loudwater, Chorleywood. *(Copyright reserved. Reproduced courtesy of the Hertfordshire Archaeological Trust.)*

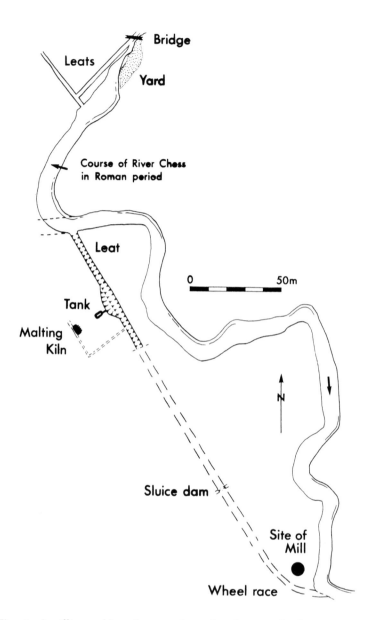

Fig.36. A milling and brewing complex at Loudwater, Chorleywood.
Special leats with a carefully designed system of sluices regulated the flow of
water to the mill. A large corn-drying oven was probably used for malting
grain for beer, and the nearby wood-lined tank used to store fresh water.
(*Drawn by Alex Thorne after Stuart Bryant, courtesy of the Hertfordshire
Archaeological Trust*).

mill fed by an extensive system of leats were excavated by Stuart Bryant, on behalf of the Hertfordshire Archaeological Trust, at Loudwater, near Rickmansworth in the south-west of the county. This particular site seems to have been a brewery, since it was provided with a large corn-drying oven and a tank, probably used to steep barley to induce it to sprout. The important point in this context is that it suggests the existence of water mills in late Roman Hertfordshire (figs. 35,36).

Other crops grown in the county were flax, beans and possibly lentils, since burnt lentils have been found as offerings in second century graves at Verulamium. Hazel nuts, cherry and plum stones and apple and blackberry pips have been found in Roman cesspits, but to what extent these fruits were cultivated rather than gathered from the wild is so far unknown.

The second element in Romano-British agriculture was animal husbandry. The evidence for this comes primarily from the animal bones found on occupation sites. Iron Age farmers raised small, short horned cattle averaging heights (to the withers) of 3ft 8ins for a cow and 4ft for a bull. Sheep also were small by modern standards, closer to the small hairy Soay sheep which survive as a specialised breed today, while horses were pony sized with an average height of 4ft 4ins (13 hands). During the four centuries of Roman rule livestock size generally increased slightly, although they were always considerably smaller than modern breeds.

Another feature of Romano-British agriculture was the gradual replacement of sheep by cattle as the most important farm animal. Cattle drew ploughs and carts, as well as providing meat, hides and bone. Pigs always provided an important secondary meat supply, and there is evidence of extensive woodlands in parts of Hertfordshire in the Roman period where pigs may have been reared. Judging by food offerings in graves, pork and poultry were the most popular meat in Roman Hertfordshire.

Of course this only gives a very generalised picture of Romano-British agriculture in the county, and we shall see in a later section that there is evidence for a certain amount of local diversity in the rural economy. In the late Iron Age wealth and power may have been measured by the number of cattle or horses a person owned, while in the later Roman period some farmers may have gone against the general trend and chosen to specialise in sheep rearing, profiting from the demand for woollen cloth.

It is clear from the map of Roman Hertfordshire on page 8 that occupation in the countryside was not spread evenly across the county. The present state of archaeological research suggests that the rural population was concentrated in three main areas, along the chalk escarpment, on the boulder clays in the north-east of the county, and in the river valleys. Away from these areas extensive tracts in what is now south-east Hertfordshire, and over the clay with flints soils on the central Chilterns, the population density seems to have been less.

The apparent variation may be partly due to the fact that less archaeological fieldwork has been carried out in south-east Hertfordshire and the central Chilterns than elsewhere in the county. Indeed recent field surveys by the Manshead Archaeological Society of Dunstable suggest that the area north-west of Luton may have supported a sizeable rural population. Nevertheless the London Clay of south-east Hertfordshire, and the clay with flints which overlie much of the south and central Chilterns both give rise to heavy, acid soils, some of which may still have been covered with dense forest in the Roman period. The discovery of the bones of red and fallow deer on several late Roman sites implies the continuing existence of forested areas throughout the Roman period. Excavation of the late Roman site at Loudwater (Chorleywood) revealed deer bones in such quantities as to raise the question whether they were deliberately farmed.

We know more about the situation on the Boulder Clays in north-east Hertfordshire thanks to an important study of the local Romano-British settlement pattern carried out by Tom Williamson. He showed that although some of the peasant settlements in this part of Hertfordshire lay on the river gravels in the valley floors, most were sited near the top of the slopes, where the lighter soils of the valley sides meet the heavier Boulder Clay on the plateau top. Such a position gave a settlement the best of all options. The lower soils were lighter and more easily drained, while those on the plateau top, although heavier, were also richer. Water supply on the upper slopes could be a problem, but the lower edge of the Boulder Clay often produced a spring line providing a handy supply of fresh water.

It looks as if the lighter soils on the valley sides were the more profitable. Williamson has suggested that settlements close to comparatively large stretches of lighter soil, for instance those on the slopes of wide and gently sloping valleys, tended to survive longer, and to produce greater quantities of more expensive pottery. In some such cases there is evidence for flint and mortar buildings, rather than timber ones. Settlements on the top of the plateau, surrounded by areas of Boulder Clay, tended to produce more coarse, locally made pottery, and to be shorter lived.

It is impossible to estimate the population of Roman Hertfordshire. Estimates for the population of Roman Britain as a whole vary between about 2.5 and 3.7 million, while, as we have seen, certain parts of Hertfordshire were more heavily populated than others. Williamson's survey in the north-east of Hertfordshire and north-west Essex recorded 35 Romano-British settlements in an area of 11 square miles. A less intensive survey, by Jonathan Hunn, in the Stevenage area of central Hertfordshire, recorded 43 Romano-British sites over 40 square miles. Certainly one benefit to local people that arose from Roman rule was that of peace, and the population probably grew in the course of the Roman period. Inter-tribal feuding ceased, and although taxes must have exerted a heavy toll, cattle and slave raiding, looting and burning, were generally things of the past.

Any rise in population however did not automatically lead to an increase in the size of individual settlements. The pattern of rural settlement in northern and central Hertfordshire, and probably elsewhere as well, was not one of villages or hamlets so much as one in which clusters of separate farmsteads were grouped around areas of intensively manured and easily worked land. This pattern has been explained as a result of a system of land holding that operated under Celtic rather than Roman law. Under Celtic inheritance law property was divided among members of an extended family, rather than simply being handed on to one or two heirs as was the case under Roman law. Celtic law tended to result in the subdivision of land, leading in time to the establishment of separate homesteads. Rather than forming a single village or hamlet, these homesteads would cluster around an area of intensively worked land, which had originally been held by a single farmstead, but which, over several generations, had become progressively fragmented. This system of land holding was not confined to the poorest classes, and there are hints of the effect of it on a number of Hertfordshire villa sites.

Early in the third century the emperor Caracalla passed an edict whereby all the freeborn people in the Roman empire were made Roman citizens. This was primarily a measure designed to make all freeborn inhabitants of the empire liable to pay taxes, which were only exacted from Roman citizens. Another effect of the edict would have been to make everyone subject to Roman rather than Celtic inheritance laws; property could now be handed on intact to a single heir. It is not known to what extent Roman law was actually observed in these rural communities, but Caracalla's edict could have had the effect of slowing down the rate at which rural holdings were being fragmented, and of encouraging the development of larger farmsteads. At all events, there seem to have been a number of different types of rural settlement. Sprawling settlements spread out over several acres, such as those south of Little Wymondley and at Pirton, existed side by side with clusters of farmsteads like those detected in the north of the county, and single farmsteads like Foxholes Farm.

The Rise and Fall of the
Hertfordshire Villa

A simple definition of the Latin word *villa* is a 'Roman house in the country.' Roman writers sometimes drew a distinction between a *villa rustica* which was likely to be a working farm, and a *villa urbana* which might be more of a luxurious country residence. In Britain, however, the term villa is generally used to describe any country house with its outbuildings (usually but not always a farm), where the main house was built according to classical architectural concepts and contained Roman features such as wall paintings, bath suites and tessellated floors. A widespread view of Roman Britain is one of a countryside liberally studded with these villas. Certainly buildings of this sort existed in what is now Hertfordshire, but they can never have formed more than a very small proportion of rural settlement.

The majority of the population lived in much humbler establishments; indeed many people in Roman Hertfordshire may never have seen the interior of a really opulent villa. To date between 30 and 35 villas are known or suspected from Hertfordshire, compared with more than 200 peasant settlements. These figures however are almost certainly misleading. Due to their greater durability and more conspicuous nature, there can be little doubt that proportionately more remains of villas have been recognised than those of humbler settlements.

Since the late 1960s a large amount of excavation has taken place on Hertfordshire villas, particularly by David Neal who has excavated four villas in the Verulamium area. As a result villas like Gorhambury, Latimer, Gadebridge and Dicket Mead are among the most extensively excavated in the country. Some grew up on the sites of farmsteads that were already thriving at the time of the Roman conquest. At Gorhambury, a short distance outside Verulamium, a farmstead had been established in the early first century when it appears to have been the residence of a local landowner. This pre-Roman farmstead comprised several buildings, including two dwelling houses, and had an imposing timber gateway implying that the place had certain social pretensions. The finds from the site, imported pottery and wine jars, also suggest that the occupants were relatively wealthy. The Roman conquest does not seem to have caused any great disruption to the life of the farm, and it was not until the Boudiccan revolt that there are hints of destruction and burning. Elsewhere occupation on pre-Roman farmsteads at Park Street, Codicote and Lockleys (Welwyn) also carried on uninterrupted by the conquest. Of course we do not know whether the same families were living on these sites before and after AD 43, but it may be significant that the old native type of buildings continued to be built on them, in preference to the new architectural styles of Rome.

It was not until the last quarter of the first century that we see 'Romanised' buildings appearing in the valleys of the Gade, Bulbourne and Chess with the construction of villas at Latimer, Northchurch, Boxmoor and Kings Langley. Although by the standards of the empire as a whole these early villas in south-west Hertfordshire were modest, they nevertheless demonstrate a degree of sophistication which until then had not been seen in the countryside and which was in many ways in advance of the standards of building in the contemporary towns. At Park Street, 3 miles south east of Verulamium, a villa with six rooms and a cellar, all resting on flint and mortar foundations, was built in the early second century. At about the same time a bath building was built, probably part of an as yet undiscovered villa, at Gadebridge (Hemel Hempstead), while at Northchurch another villa also seems to have been provided with a bath house (fig. 37).

The most luxurious of these early villas was at Gorhambury. Here the second century villa had five rooms as well as a projecting wing at one end. The house was decorated with painted stucco mouldings, while fragments of mosaic floors and painted plaster ceilings reflect the owner's determination to parade, not just his wealth, but also his appreciation of Roman fashion and style. During the course of the second century the fashion for comfortable country houses spread, and villas were often embellished with tessellated floors, and plastered and painted walls became common. By the end of the century villas were also spreading over a wider area, and were tending to become rather larger. Excavations

Fig.37. Reconstruction of the Northchurch villa in the 2nd century.
(Copyright St Albans Museums).

in the north of the county, in advance of a bypass near Little
Wymondley, located the remains of a small 'cottage' villa built in
the late first or early second century. Although it had only four
rooms on the ground floor, the walls rested on flint and mortar
footings, and it seems to have had both a tiled roof and a
tessellated pavement. A century later a flint and mortar wall was
added, enclosing an area of about 500 square yards; it is not
clear whether this supported a large hall, barn or workshops, or
whether it enclosed a courtyard, but clearly the villa was a
flourishing concern.

Unbroken prosperity however was not something that was
enjoyed by all Hertfordshire villa owners. Indeed their fortunes
showed a marked tendency to fluctuate in the course of the Roman
period, and this was particularly the case in the south-west of the
county. The third century seems to have been an especially uncertain time, with several villas suffering a marked decline in the early
years of the century, and again between about 275 and 300.

Fig.38. Excavating the early-4th century swimming pool at Gadebridge
Villa. *(Copyright St Albans Museums, and courtesy David Neal).*

The early fourth century saw a brief revival. New villas were
built in the north of the county at Radwell, and at Standon (near
Braughing), while the villas at Moor Park (near Watford), Park
Street and Latimer were rebuilt. Other villas were repaired or ex-
tended. Gorhambury was refurbished at the end of the third century and Dicket Mead (Welwyn) which had first been built in
about 200, was extended. A remarkable feature of some of the late
Roman Hertfordshire villas was the provision of swimming pools.
Open air pools were dug at Kings Langley, Boxmoor and Great
Wymondley. All these were dwarfed however by the enormous
pool that was constructed at the Gadebridge villa in about 325.
This was 40ft wide and 68ft 6in long and was entered by a flight of
five steps (fig. 38).

For some villa dwellers this upsurge in fortunes did not last and
by the middle of the fourth century many villas were in terminal

decline. Although those at Radwell, Wymondley, Moor Park and possibly Park Street continued to flourish until the very end of the Roman period, Lockleys was abandoned in the middle of the fourth century, while the standard of living at Gorhambury, Gadebridge, Dicket Mead and Latimer drastically declined. The 'cottage' villa at Little Wymondley had been unoccupied since the end of the third century, although it is possible that a new villa had been built close by. Nevertheless by the end of the fourth century the whole site seems to have been deserted (fig.39).

Fig.39. Ground plans of some Hertfordshire villas. The plans of Park Street and Lockleys are those of simple 'cottage' villas and date from the late 1st century. Gadebridge, Gorhambury and Childwick are examples of 2nd and 3rd century corridor villas, while the plans of Dicket Mead and Latimer represent two of the largest late Roman villas from the county. (*Drawn by Alex Thorne*).

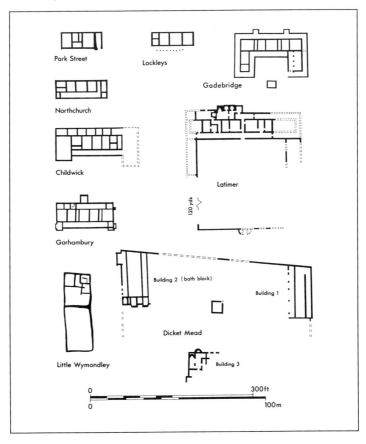

Villas were often planned with a varying number of rooms opening off a corridor, sometimes with projecting wings at each end.
Several had basements, and some may have had an upper storey as
well. By the fourth century a few had become larger still, and as in
the case of Gadebridge and Latimer the projecting wings had been
extended to enclose the sides of a courtyard or garden.

The occupants clearly took pride in the appearance of their
houses. At Gadebridge an elegant facade was added in the fourth
century, designed to give the house an imposing aspect, while at
about the same time a similar facade was added to the neighbouring Boxmoor villa, this one apparently designed to impress passing
travellers on Akeman Street.

Similar care and expense was applied to the interiors. At Gorhambury realistically painted life-sized human figures in stucco
work decorated the first century dining room at a time when such
things were unknown, even in nearby Verulamium. By the middle
of the next century wall paintings and mosaics had become relatively common, although unfortunately only a few small fragments survive. Most villas had at least one room heated by a
hypocaust, which drew hot air from a furnace through channels
under the floor and up the walls, to escape through vents beneath
the eaves. Individual rooms heated in this way were probably
dining or reception rooms, but in several villas a whole series of
heated rooms have been recorded; these must represent bath
suites, built on lines similar to those of public baths, but on a
smaller scale. In some villas the baths occupied a wing of the
house but in others they were housed in separate bath blocks.
Remains of one were excavated at Dicket Mead, and thanks to the
enterprise of the excavator, Tony Rook, it has been preserved in a
specially built dome beneath the A1(M) motorway at Welwyn, and
is open to visitors. Laid out beneath the motorway are the third
century foundations of the hot room, warm room and cold room,
with the base of the cold plunge pool still in position (fig.40).

The villas of Hertfordshire never seem to have reached the
affluence displayed by some elsewhere in Britain. The enormous,
luxurious late Roman villas of the Cotswolds and Somerset have
no counterparts in Hertfordshire. Nevertheless the difference between a rich Hertfordshire villa like Standon, Gorhambury or
Gadebridge, and an average peasant settlement like Foxholes

Fig.40. Dicket Mead bath house, preserved under the A1(M). In the foreground is the tiled floor of the unheated dressing room. In the background is the base of the hot water boiler with a large flue beneath it leading directly to the furnace behind. In front of the boiler are the piles of tiles which once supported the raised floor of the hot room, while to the left of the boiler are the remains of the plaster lined hot bath. *(Copyright Mill Green Museum, Hatfield).*

Farm was pronounced. The occupants of the villas in the county may not have been millionaires, nor the peasants mere subsistence farmers, but the gulf between the two was wide.

Who the occupants of villas were is a question which archaeologists find extremely difficult to answer. Some, particularly in the early years of Roman rule, must still have been the homes of local aristocratic families who continued to farm their ancestral land. Several farmsteads which started life in the pre-Roman period, in time developed into comfortable Roman villas, and the absence of any signs of destruction suggests a peaceful transition from Celtic state to Roman province. This development seems to have started particularly early in the Verulamium region, where villas at Lockleys, Park Street and Gorhambury were built within two generations of the conquest. Whether the same families were occupying these farms as in the pre-Roman period is another matter, but the assumption is that they were.

A glance at the map of Roman Hertfordshire on page 8 will show that, like the peasant settlements, the villas are not distributed evenly across the county, but occur in distinct clusters. They tend to be commoner around towns; thus there are remains of two known or suspected villas within 3 miles of Verulamium, two within a similar distance of Baldock, one on the outskirts of Braughing, and two within 2 miles of Cow Roast. This phenomenon has been observed elsewhere in Roman Britain, and it is generally agreed that those close to major towns were probably the homes of native landowning families from whose ranks the town council members were drawn. The villas close to smaller towns (like Braughing) may have housed local administrators responsible for running these smaller units.

As the Roman period advanced, so individuals who had started life in humble circumstances were sometimes able to improve their lot to the extent of being able to invest their wealth in land, so that occasionally even people whose parents were slaves, or who had been slaves themselves, could amass considerable fortunes. We know of one Catuvellaunian woman, Regina, who although originally a slave, had married a successful Greek standard (or flag) maker. Regina died at the comparatively young age of 30, but it is clear from her tombstone at Chesters on Hadrian's Wall, that she was already a well-to-do provincial matron. No doubt Regina was just one of many Catuvellaunian people who prospered under

Roman rule in spite of servile origins. Some of these no doubt built themselves comfortable villas in Hertfordshire. It is noticeable that areas of pottery or tile production tend to also have a number of villas 'clustering' round them. Are these the homes of the local elite who invested some of their wealth in pottery production and used the proceeds to embellish their houses, or are they the homes of successful craftsmen who had amassed wealth in the potteries and tileries? We shall never know the answer, but both possibilities have to be borne in mind.

There is therefore no simple answer to the question who lived in the Hertfordshire villas. Some no doubt were occupied by the descendants of the original tribal aristocracy, but as the Roman period progressed more and more were probably occupied by people who were originally craftsmen or peasant farmers. Some may have owned their villas, but others may have rented them, perhaps from a distant landlord. Other villas may have been run by bailiffs, and it is even possible that in the late Roman period some Hertfordshire land was owned by the emperor, and managed by tenants or agents. Certainly the discovery on two south Hertfordshire villa sites (Latimer and Gadebridge) of lead seals of the type used to mark imperial property suggests that by the fourth century these particular villas may have been farmed on behalf of the central government.

EVERYDAY LIFE IN THE VILLAS

In spite of the evidence for comfort and even luxury, the Hertfordshire villas were working establishments. Elegant interior decoration and elaborate facades no doubt impressed visitors, but to keep things going the owners had to make money. Most villas were farms, but some must also have profited from industry. The villas around Park Street and Radlett, south of Verulamium, must have benefited from the pottery industry that flourished here in the late first and second centuries. Traces of timber on the banks of the Ver behind the villa at Park Street have been interpreted as the remain of a wharf, and it is possible that pots made in nearby kilns were transported by barge to markets elsewhere. The villas at Northchurch and Berkhamsted are close to the important iron working area at Cow Roast, which no doubt provided their owners' income. The occupants of the Dicket Mead villa probably owed their wealth to the rich arable land in central Hertfordshire, although it is possible that they supplemented their income by dealing in expensive sculpture which was imported from the Mediterranean in a half completed state, and 'finished' on the banks of the Mimram.

Farming was the mainstay of the rural economy, and the distribution of Hertfordshire villas echoes that of the peasant settlements, and reflects the areas of farmland (as opposed to woodland) in the Roman period. Unfortunately, in the past, excavators of Roman villas tended to concentrate on the main dwelling house, paying relatively little attention to the outbuildings, workshops, barns and fields. In recent years attempts have been made to rectify this, but we still know less about the farm buildings and farmland surrounding the villas than we do about the villas themselves.

In the south-west of the county the spacing of villas in the valleys of the Chess, Bulbourne, Gade and Ver has led to the suggestion that they were built about one and a half miles apart. The size of the estates associated with them is extremely difficult to estimate. It has been calculated that the granary at the Gorhambury villa would have stored up to about 88,000 lb. of wheat, a yield requiring 750 acres to produce. In an unmechanised age this sort of acreage would have required about 35 people to work it, giving a total population for an average sized villa of 60-80 people (allowing for young children, aged relatives etc.). Clearly provision had to be made for the housing of these farm workers as well as for the family of the owner. The Gorhambury villa had its own bath house, which was presumably reserved for the use of the family, but in an outer compound, and separate from any other dwelling house, there was a second bath house. It has been suggested that this was used by the farm workers. About half a mile to the north of the villa traces of a typical peasant settlement made up of ditched pens, enclosures and droveways have been recorded on aerial photographs. Was this the settlement in which the Gorhambury farm workers lived, making periodic visits to the outer Gorhambury compound for a bath? A similar system may have operated 4 miles away at Park Street, where again, two bath blocks were built, one separated from the villa itself.

In the north of the county several peasant settlements are known within a mile of a villa, suggesting that here again farm workers lived in a neighbouring hamlet or small settlement. Precisely how the arrangement worked we have no means of knowing, but it is clear that villas and peasant settlements were closely connected. The one at Little Wymondley in north Hertfordshire stood close to the River Beane, but to the south of it Roman roofing tiles and pottery have been noted over an area of some twenty acres, and presumably this debris marks the site of the estate workers' quarters.

A final point in connection with Hertfordshire villas is the presence on a number of sites of two dwelling houses. At Radwell, two stood at right angles to each other on two sides of a yard. At Park Street two villas occupied the site in the late second century. At Welwyn, two villas, Lockleys and Dicket Mead, grew up within 100 yards of each other on either side of the Mimram, although it is by no means certain that both were occupied simultaneously. It has also been suggested that the large villa at Gadebridge was a double house in the sense that it had two entrance porches and duplicate sets of rooms, the west side of the house mirroring the east. J.T. Smith has suggested that these double and dual villas reflect the Celtic system of inheritance under which a property was split equally between heirs. This theory has not received universal acceptance among archaeologists, partly on the grounds that if such a system operated among villa owners, the phenomenon of double and dual villas would be more widespread, and not simply confined to a few rather sporadic instances. Alternative explanations for this doubling up of villas could be that it is the result of a house being built for the heir to the property during the lifetime of the owner, or to house a bailiff or manager.

The Economic Base

TRADE

One of the results of the Roman conquest was a dramatic increase in the volume of trade, not only between Britain and the Continent, but also between different parts of Britain itself, as well as within the Catuvellaunian area. Before the coming of Rome the organisation of trading ventures between the Continent and southern Britain must have been a complicated operation. Not only did a continental merchant have to raise the capital for the goods, but carriers, packhorses, ships and crew, and perhaps even guards for slaves would all have had to be arranged. Added to this, the existence in south Britain, of numerous tribes, not all of them equally well disposed towards foreigners, probably meant that bribes and gifts had to be made in order to ensure a safe passage.

All this changed under Roman rule. The construction of a comprehensive road system, the provision of harbours, wharfs and lighthouses, and above all the maintenance of peace, must have removed many of the dangers and uncertainties of trading missions. No less important was the presence in Britain of the Roman army, creating a permanent body of people with regular pay and demanding a constant supply of goods and services.

With the growth of trade a whole range of new goods from all over the Roman empire became available in Hertfordshire. Increasingly exotic goods, previously the monopoly of the tribal elite, were within the reach of many local families. Although most household pottery continued to be made locally, Samian ware, a glossy red tableware imported from France, has been found in relatively modest settlements (fig.41). Glassware and clay figurines were mass produced in large workshops on the Rhine, and these too are found on comparatively humble farmsteads as well as in the homes of the better off. There is evidence that the inhabitants of Verulamium were able to indulge in wine from Egypt, dates from Palestine, and emeralds from Egypt.

Although Roman rule brought a prolonged period of peace, long suffering peasants presumably had to satisfy the demands of the tax collector as well as those of landlord or patron. However reasonably priced imports may have been, they all had to be paid for, ultimately either out of agricultural surpluses or their by-products, or by manufacturing goods from local materials. The tribal elite must also have found that the establishment of Roman peace was by no means an unmitigated blessing. One profitable source of income must now have been denied them, that of raiding neighbouring territories for cattle and slaves. In addition to paying taxes, tribal leaders were expected to finance public works and services, such as the construction of monumental arches or the provision of public spectacles in the theatre. Such considerations must have provided every incentive to improve agricultural and manufacturing techniques and to specialise in products for which there was a ready market. Although pottery and tile manufacture and iron working were important, the mainstay of the economy of Roman Hertfordshire was agriculture and its by-products. Along with the rest of the Romano-British population, the great majority of the Catuvellauni still relied on agriculture for their livelihood.

Fig.41.   A samian ware bowl decorated with fighting gladiators. *(Copyright St Albans Museums).*

There is growing evidence to suggest that as the Roman period progressed so the opportunities provided by a wider market led to a certain amount of diversification and specialisation among Hertfordshire farmers. Before the Roman period corn was artificially dried in order to stop it sprouting during storage, but gradually more efficient corn-drying ovens became widespread across the county. Agricultural tools were improved and the introduction of hay as a crop made it easier to keep farm animals over the winter, and enabled improvements to be made to the breeding stock.

Dozens of corn-drying ovens have been recorded from the county. Although the presence of one or two ovens on a farmstead may simply reflect the requirements of a normal mixed farm, some sites have produced multiple corn-drying ovens and suggest specialisation in corn production. At Verulamium, for example, 6 ovens have been recorded over the years, and at Foxholes Farm 5 ovens were excavated in the 1970s. In the north of the county at Wymondley, a large number of querns as well as a winnowing floor and corn-drying oven suggest similar specialisation. At Gorhambury remains of a tower granary have been excavated, capable of storing an estimated 88,000 lb. of wheat. Another possible example was excavated by Sir Mortimer Wheeler inside Verulamium and recently two small granaries were uncovered in the centre of the town; these had been burned down in the fire of 155 and piles of burnt wheat were found still heaped on the raised floors.

Elsewhere in the county sheep farming seems to have been profitable, especially in the third and fourth centuries when British cloth enjoyed a widespread reputation. Tom Williamson's work has led to the suggestion that the most profitable land on the light soils of the valley slopes in the north east of the county was used for sheep rearing. Animal bones found at Baldock and Braughing also suggest that the farmers of north Hertfordshire favoured sheep, in contrast to the general swing in late Roman Britain towards raising cattle.

Supporting evidence for the importance of cloth manufacture comes from Verulamium. Here a large third century house contained several mortar lined tanks, similar to examples from France which are thought to have been used for dying cloth. Two more tanks just outside the town may also have been used for fulling or

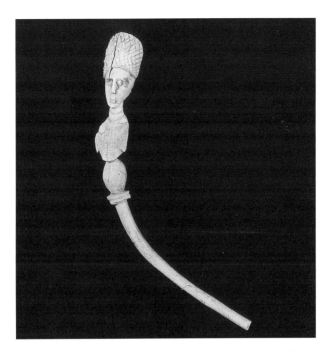

Fig. 42. A fine demonstration of local bone-carvers' skill. This hair pin is minutely decorated with a woman's head showing the elaborate hairstyle fashionable in the late-1st century. *(Copyright St Albans Museums)*.

dyeing, and the same site produced part of a large iron wool-carding comb and two small bone weaving combs. Another wool-carding comb was found at the nearby Gorhambury site.

Another agricultural by-product in constant demand in the Roman world was leather. Tanning and leather-working were highly profitable trades as leather was used by all sections of the population, not only for footwear but for horse equipment and clothing, while the army created the greatest demand, since they also needed leather for tents and uniforms. Tanning is a smelly and unpleasant process, so at Verulamium it is hardly surprising to find that it was carried on a short distance outside the town. Alongside the tanners, highly profitable subsidiary enterprises flourished; bone workers manufactured pins, needles and spoons, while tallow renderers used animal fat to produce cheap candles, and leather workers cut and stitched the hides (fig.42).

Many crafts, particularly those practised in rural districts, have left little or no trace. The river valleys must have produced large

Above Fig.43. A mortarium or mixing bowl. *(Copyright St Albans Museums).*

Above right Fig.44. The bird-catcher at work. Birds were popular pets in the Roman world. On this intaglio from Verulamium, a countryman is using a net at the end of a pole to catch a bird in a tree. A basketwork bird cage is at the man's feet. *(Copyright St Albans Museums).*

quantities of rushes and willows, and there can be no doubt that basketry was a local craft. There is ample evidence for the popularity of basket chairs in Roman Britain, as well as baskets and rush matting, but archaeological remains of this industry are non-existent (fig.43).

POTTERY

The commonest find on Romano-British sites in Hertfordshire is pottery, the bulk of which was made locally. No sooner had the county been absorbed into the Roman empire than immigrant potters arrived bringing with them new techniques, types of kiln and styles of pottery. These quickly replaced the established native forms, and by the end of the first century were flooding the markets of south-east England.

The immigrant potters originated in Gaul, and arrived here shortly after the conquest in the wake of the Roman army. We know the names of some of them from their habit of stamping their names on some of their products, particularly on large mixing bowls or *mortaria* (fig.44). A whole range of vessels were produced including amphorae, which were often used for storing wine; this raises the question whether vines were cultivated in Roman Hertfordshire. A study of the names stamped on *mortaria* has led to the identification of the Romano-British name for Bricket Wood, the area where these vessels were manufactured. Bricket Wood today is a sizeable village south-east of St Albans; in the first century AD it was known as Lugdunum.

The earliest Romano-British kilns were established near Verulamium in about AD 50. By the end of the first century kilns were also operating some 10 miles south along Watling Street at Brockley Hill just outside Stanmore (fig. 45). Brockley Hill was known as Salonicae, which means 'the estate belonging to Salonicus'. Salonicae consisted of a number of kilns, and it has been suggested that this was an industrial estate, perhaps run by slaves, and that Salonicus himself was an immigrant potter for Gaul. At any event, the Verulamium/Salonicae pottery industry reached its peak between about AD 70 and 140; it started to decline

Fig.45. A Roman pottery kiln. The stokehole and furnace were in the foreground. The plinth within the round kiln supported a raised floor on which the pots were placed. *(Copyright St Albans Museums).*

in the later second century, and although it staggered on until the middle of the third century, by the fourth century it had been superseded by a pottery industry that had grown up in central and eastern Hertfordshire, centred around Hadham.

Kilns had already been established in central Hertfordshire in the pre-Roman period, centred on Welwyn and Ware, but the industry only really took off there in the third century; by the fourth century it was the most important pottery industry in the county, supplying most of the local communities and exporting pots to Essex, London and Northampton.

There can be little doubt that the Hertfordshire pottery industries operated from rural estates rather than from towns. Although a few kilns are known or suspected from Verulamium in the first and second centuries, their distribution in the second to fourth is predominantly rural, influenced no doubt by the existence of suitable clay deposits and wood to fire them. The presence of good roads and navigable waterways to transport the bulky but fragile goods must have been an added consideration. Successful potters no doubt used their profits to embellish their houses, which is why several Hertfordshire villas cluster around the pottery producing areas.

Closely associated with the pottery industry was the tile industry. The new styles of building introduced at the time of the conquest ensured a constant demand for tile and brick, and impressive tile kilns like that excavated at Park Street are widespread in the county.

QUARRIES

Building materials of all sorts constituted another source of income for Romano-British entrepreneurs. Major building schemes such as the construction of the Verulamium town walls would have demanded vast quantities of flint and mortar. Flint was probably mined in Roman Hertfordshire; later flint mines are known from the county, although none has yet been recognised from the Roman period. Chalk would have been needed for lime mortar, and Roman chalk quarries are known from Pirton and Verulamium.

For facings and for high status buildings, stone had to be imported from elsewhere. Purbeck marble from Dorset, and sandstone from Northampton and oolitic limestone from the Cotswolds have been recorded on Roman sites in Hertfordshire. Evidence has been found suggesting that a firm of monumental masons was importing marble from Greece and producing highly competent statues and facings on the villa site at Dicket Mead.

A locally occurring stone that was commercially exploited was Hertfordshire pudding stone. This is an exceptionally hard con-glomerate that occurs naturally in the south-west of the county. It was used for querns, which were traded across southern England, but the centre for the trade is still waiting to be recognised.

METAL WORKING

Iron working was already a major Hertfordshire industry at the time of the Roman conquest. At Cow Roast, between Berkhamsted and Tring, iron workings covered more than 10 square kilometres. Here iron ore occurred naturally in the clay and flint. The ore was first roasted, then smelted in iron furnaces, several of which have been excavated in recent years. The Cow Roast iron works pre-sumably provided the wealth behind a number of comfortable villas in the Berkhamsted/Tring area, but iron working depended on large quantities of charcoal to fuel the furnaces, and by the fourth century activity at Cow Roast seems to have been declining. It may be that centuries of charcoal burning had led to drastic deforestation, and a consequent decline in the local industry.

Romano-British iron working was not confined to the Cow Roast area. Small scale iron working was widespread in the county, and probably every settlement had its own blacksmith, many of whom probably used locally smelted iron. So far, how-ever, no other site in the county has produced evidence for iron working on the scale of that at Cow Roast.

Bronze and copper working was also widespread although, unlike iron, the ore was not available locally. Most of the bronze and copper was probably smelted elsewhere and imported into the county in the form of ingots. Metal from ingots was aug-mented by the use of scrap metal; unwanted or broken objects that were melted down and re-used. The Verulamium Venus, one of the finest bronze statuettes from the county, was discovered in a second century bronze worker's shop among a pile of scrap metal waiting to be melted down (see frontispiece illustration).

Fig.46. A lead ingot from Cheshunt. The moulded inscription reads IMP. CAES. HADRIANI AUG. (belonging to the emperor Caesar Hadrian Augustus). This dates the ingot to the reign of Hadrian, AD117-138. *(Copyright British Museum).*

Bronze and copper smiths were active in most if not all of the small settlements. One bronzesmith working at Braughing in the third century specialised in producing brooches for the local community, and a similar workshop has been recorded at Baldock. Although some of the products are somewhat crude, many demonstrate not only the skill of the local smiths, but also the persistence of Celtic art styles throughout the Roman period.

Lead was widely used for tanks, pipes and, especially in the late Roman period, for coffins. It was also a principal source of silver in the Roman world. A lead ingot weighing 184 lb, found in the 19th century close to Ermine Street at Cheshunt, was stamped with the emperor Hadrian's name, and probably came from the lead mines in Derbyshire. The letters 'xx' inscribed on the ingot possibly refer to the 20th Legion, which may have been working the lead mines at the time (fig.46).

Religion

Religion, magic and superstition played a central role in the everyday lives of the people of Roman Hertfordshire, but sadly this is one of the most difficult areas of the past to interpret. It is one thing to detect the outward trappings of religion, the temples, sanctuaries and votive offerings, but quite another to understand the beliefs of those who produced them. The problem of course is made immeasurably more difficult by the absence of written records.

Julius Caesar, writing about the continental Celts, remarked that 'the whole nation is greatly devoted to ritual observances'. Caesar's description is supported by the findings of modern archaeologists, and there can be no doubt that the Catuvellauni were deeply concerned with supernatural forces. A few sacred sites, dating from shortly before the Roman conquest, have been recognised in Hertfordshire, and these provide a glimpse of native religious practices before they were overlain by ideas based on the religion of Greece and Rome.

SACRED SITES

In the later part of the first century BC we find the first of the religious centres, which, while their origins were firmly planted in the pre-Roman Iron Age, nevertheless continued to flourish during the Roman period. Such centres arc known or suspected at Essendon and Braughing, and less certainly at Flamstead. Like most pre-Roman Celtic sanctuaries they contained no buildings, but were primarily meeting places consisting of a ditched enclosure surrounding a central area from which the uninitiated may well have been excluded. It is possible that trees or sacred groves once stood within the enclosures, and occasionally deep pits or ponds have been found.

There is convincing evidence that sacrifices played an important role in Celtic ceremonies; indeed one of the most effective punishments commonly meted out was to ban someone from attending sacrifices. A variety of goods were given as sacrificial offerings, particularly tools, implements, weapons, brooches and coins, but human and animal sacrifices were by no means uncommon. Sometimes offerings were simply heaped up within a sacred enclosure; the fear of offending a powerful god was sufficient to deter any pilferers.

At Braughing, human and animal bones have been excavated in ditches surrounding the enclosure; bones which may well be those of offerings made at the sanctuary. Another ditched enclosure, just across the Essex border at Harlow, surrounded a shallow pond into which offerings were probably thrown. For centuries the Celtic tribes both in Britain and on the Continent had been venerating springs, rivers and marshes, and throwing offerings into them. Deep pits, symbolising openings or gateways into the spirit world, were also thought appropriate places to make offerings to the gods, and pits are frequently found in Celtic sanctuaries.

THE GODS OF THE CATUVELLAUNI

The Celts worshipped literally hundreds of different gods and goddesses. Every tribe or group had its own god, Toutatis or Toutates, an 'all rounder' who was probably originally the tribal ancestor and who protected the tribe. Other Celtic deities were specifically connected with particular aspects of life; healing gods, smith gods, fertility gods and gods associated with certain animals, birds or natural features like springs and rivers. One that appears to have been particularly popular among the Catuvellauni was a warrior god, often depicted as a horseman. Several small brooches showing him mounted, armed with a spear and wearing a crested helmet, have been found in Verulamium (fig.47). At Brigstock (Northamptonshire) in the northern part of the Catuvellaunian territory, there was a major cult centre dedicated to the horse-riding warrior god. The Catuvellauni certainly seem to have worshipped a warrior god, who in the Roman period was probably equated with Mars, the Roman god of war. In the mid-18th century a hoard of Romano-British bronze and silver objects was found near Barkway, in north Hertfordshire, about a mile east of Ermine Street. The hoard consisted of a small bronze

Fig.47. A bronze brooch, inlaid with enamel, in the shape of a horse-riding warrior. The warrior's spear is broken off, but his crested helmet can still be made out. *(Drawn by Alex Thorne).*

statuette of Mars and seven silver plaques in the shape of stylised leaves. These objects were probably originally displayed in a nearby temple, and may have been deliberately hidden for safety, possibly by cult members anxious to save them from Christian iconoclasts in the late Roman period. The statuette is of Mars, and four of the silver plaques also carried his image, complete with helmet, spear and shield. One of the most interesting objects in the hoard however, is a fifth plaque carrying a simple inscription 'To Mars Toutatis, Titus Claudius Primus, freedman of Attius, fulfils his promise'. The double name god, Mars Toutatis, reflects a common Romano-British practice whereby a native deity was matched to the nearest Roman equivalent. In this way Toutatis, the tribal god of the Catuvellauni, was equated with the Roman god of war, Mars. The remaining two plaques from Barkway show Vulcan, the Roman god of smiths, but although the Barkway Vulcan looks very like a Roman deity, the Celts also worshipped a smith god, and in Hertfordshire, where iron working was so important both in the Roman and the pre-Roman periods, the two gods may well have been equated in the same way as Mars and Toutatis were (fig. 48).

Fig.48. A silver plaque from Barkway showing the smith god, Vulcan. (*Copyright British Museum*).

THE GODS OF ROME

One of the major effects of the Roman conquest was the exposure of local people to new ideas and influences. As soon as the Catuvellaunian kingdom was drawn into the Roman empire it was immediately opened up to traders, officials and speculators from all corners of the empire. All these diverse peoples brought with them their own religious beliefs.

On the whole the Romans were genuinely tolerant of religious beliefs; they only drew the line at human sacrifice and at cults that were regarded as subversive. Christians tended to be persecuted because their refusal to sacrifice to the official gods on state occasions was taken as an indication that they did not support Roman rule. In addition to the welter of religions brought in by the army and traders, the Roman government introduced the state religion of Rome. The most important Roman gods were Jupiter, Juno and Minerva who, as the guardian gods of Rome, formed the focus of the Roman state religion. Side by side with these, the emperor himself tended to be worshipped as a god. On a large number of occasions in the year, such as the emperor's birthday, town magistrates all over the empire would be required to conduct public sacrifices to ensure the continued safety of emperor and state. These would take place in the forum, and it is probable that the three temples that stood on the south side of the forum at Verulamium were dedicated to the state gods of Rome and to the emperor.

The most popular deities in Roman Hertfordshire were Mercury (god of trade and crafts) and Mars (god of war). As bringer of good fortune, Mercury, like Mars, was often equated with Toutatis, and he was certainly a popular deity in Verulamium, where fragments of five statuettes or engravings of him have been found. The finest of these shows the god accompanied by a ram, a tortoise and a cock (all traditional associates of Mercury) and was found just outside the town walls. Although this little statue is entirely Classical in style, Mercury is wearing a miniature silver torc around his neck. Torcs were symbols of power in the Celtic world, and the presence of one here underlines the continuing Celtic aspect of this highly Romanised representation (fig.49).

Mercury's female counterpart was Minerva (goddess of wisdom) who was often equated with the Celtic goddess Rosmerta. Minerva/Rosmerta seems to have been worshipped alongside Mercury at Harlow, and it is possible that she was also worshipped at Verulamium. Here a small bronze model of an owl, Minerva's attribute, was found associated with a Romano-Celtic temple which marked the site of the first century royal burial at Folly Lane. The Folly Lane temple is also an indication that the first century ruler buried here continued to be venerated as a hero or guardian of the tribe; for most of the Roman period worship of semi-divine heroes went on alongside that of the gods. Another outstanding Romano-British statuette also comes from Verulamium; the so-called Verulamium Venus. In fact this goddess may not be Venus at all but Persephone, a goddess of fertility and the underworld. In her right hand she holds what appears to be a pomegranate, a traditional attribute of Persephone, and unlike Venus who was generally naked, she is partially clothed.

The Roman historian Tacitus tells us that the sons of British noblemen were particularly keen to try anything new, but there is no reason to suppose that this appreciation of fresh ideas was confined to the upper classes. Certainly there is plenty of evidence

Left Fig.49. A bronze statuette of Mercury from Verulamium. The god, accompanied by a ram, cock and tortoise, was found with a miniature silver torc round his neck. *(Copyright St Albans Museums).*

Below Fig.50. Reconstruction of the Triangular Temple, Verulamium. This temple was probably dedicated to the eastern goddess Cybele. *(From a painting by Alan Sorrell.)*

to show that new religious cults were being adopted throughout the Roman period.

The triangular temple at Verulamium (so called because of its unusual plan) lay at the south entrance to the late first century town, and seems to have been dedicated to Cybele, a near Eastern fertility goddess who was popular in Britain in the second and third centuries (fig.50). An inscription on a pot found in a grave at Dunstable, 10 miles along Watling Street, tells us that the jar was dedicated to the dead person by a man called Regillinus, on behalf of fellow worshippers of Cybele. Other followers of exotic religions are known from their lost property. Early in the third century a follower of the Persian god of light, Mithras, dropped a Mithraic amulet near the Verulamium theatre, while a cornelian signet ring engraved with the head of the Egyptian god Serapis was dropped on the Colchester road in about AD 200. The amulet worn to protect women in childbirth that was found at Dicket Mead, Welwyn, has already been mentioned.

During the Roman period temples and shrines were built in the county for the first time, although many of them occupied sites that were already sacred in earlier centuries. Most of the temples consisted of a square or rectangular building, the *cella*, which was surrounded by a portico or verandah. The *cella* was a shrine which housed the cult object, probably a statue of the god, while the verandah was used to display offerings or inscriptions recording promises and thank offerings. Silver leaves, like those found at Barkway in north Hertfordshire, were often nailed up in temple verandahs as thank offerings, while bronze letters, like some found on the villa site at Dicket Mead (Welwyn), may once have formed part of a dedicatory inscription outside a local shrine (fig.51). Curses inscribed on lead plaques, usually asking the god to punish thieves and restore stolen property, were also nailed up in temple verandahs (fig.52).

Romano-Celtic temples were scattered across the county, both in towns and the countryside, and would have been the places where most people worshipped their gods. Classical temples were normally only found in towns. Temples formed the public face of the religious life of the people, but most households would also have had their own private shrine, either tucked away in the back room behind a shop in a modest household, or occupying a central position in an aristocratic residence. Here the head of the household would make daily offerings of food and drink to the family gods (fig.53).

Fig.51. Bronze letters from the villa at Dicket Mead, Welwyn. (*Copyright Mill Green Museum, Hatfield*).

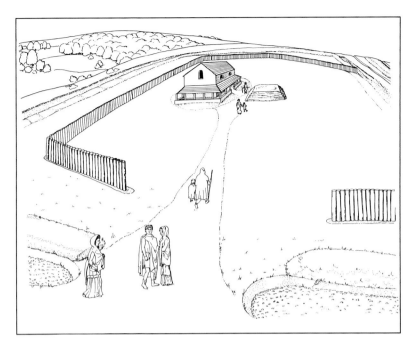

Fig.52.   Imaginative reconstruction of the Romano-Celtic temple near the royal burial site at Folly Lane, Verulamium. *(Drawn by Alex Thorne)*.

Fig.53.   A 'mother goddess' from Baldock. Female deities brought health and good fortune and were popular all over the Celtic provinces of the Roman empire: clay figurines like this one were mass produced in factories on the Rhine. *(Copyright North Herts District Council Museums Service)*.

Without doubt the most important religion to be introduced into the county during the Roman period was Christianity, but although there is clear evidence for a Christian community at Verulamium evidence for Christians elsewhere in the county is rather scanty.

Verulamium was the scene of the martyrdom of the earliest British martyr, St Alban. Alban, an inhabitant of Verulamium, sheltered a Christian priest during a period of persecution, probably early in the third century. Having himself been converted by the priest, Alban refused to take part in official sacrifices, which led to a charge of subversion against the state being brought against him. He was found guilty and executed a short distance outside the town. Traditionally the site of his martyrdom is placed where St Albans Abbey now stands, and indeed the presence of a late Roman cemetery close to the Abbey lends weight to this tradition.

Remains of what appear to be two Roman churches are known from the Roman town itself. One was excavated on the site of a cemetery dating from the third and fourth centuries a few yards outside the London Gate, and the other lay near the south corner of the town and was excavated in 1935. The remains of both buildings lay close to the modern surface and had been badly damaged, so that their identification is uncertain. However the form of both is similar to that of early Christian churches. Remarkably the only other evidence for Christianity in Verulamium comes from a few words scratched on pots or utensils, such as *Vivante*, which was a traditional early Christian phrase meaning 'may you have eternal life'.

Evidence for Christianity in the rest of Hertfordshire during the Roman period is even more scanty. A bronze finger ring found at the late Roman villa at Moor Park was inscribed with a design of two doves on a palm branch, which are both early Christian symbols. Another late Roman villa, at Northchurch, produced fragments of painted wall plaster, and it has been suggested that the design originally included a *chi rho* monogram; *chi* and *rho* are the first two letters of Christ's name in the Greek alphabet. Sometimes the monogram itself was flanked by an *alpha* and *omega*, which as the first and last letters of the Greek alphabet signified Christ at the beginning and end of life. The Northchurch plaster fragment may include part of the *alpha* from this type of symbol.

Burial Rituals in Roman Hertfordshire

Well over 7,000 Roman burials are known from Hertfordshire. Many were found close to towns, but others represent the inhabitants of rural settlements and villas. In the early Roman period the predominant burial rite was cremation – the ashes of the dead were buried either in a pottery jar or in some other container made of a perishable material such as leather, textile or wood. The ashes were often accompanied by 'grave offerings' – gifts of food, drink or personal possessions which the dead person might need on the journey to the afterlife (fig.54). The quantity and quality of the offerings presumably reflect the wealth or generosity of the surviving friends and relatives. One cremation burial from Baldock contained 31 oil lamps. Was this person's funeral attended by 31 friends, each of whom left a lamp to lighten the journey to the afterlife?

A more sinister find in another Baldock grave was a lead plaque inscribed with a curse. This is an example of a practice occasionally noted from Romano-British graves, whereby a curse was placed in the grave as a request to the gods of the underworld. The actual wording of the Baldock curse is indecipherable, but it concerns a woman called Tacita, and had been written backwards to increase its magical potency.

By the third century cremation had been largely replaced by inhumation, and by the fourth century the practice of providing grave offerings had declined, perhaps due to the influence of Christianity. Wealthy individuals however might be buried in expensive stone or lead coffins (fig.55).

A few graves were marked by elaborate tombs or *mausolea*. Remains of marble *mausolea* have been found at Welwyn and St Albans, while at Harpenden and Woodlane End near Hemel Hempstead temple-like shrines marked what were probably the family burial grounds of landowning families. At Woodlane End

Fig. 54. A collection of grave offerings from a burial outside Verulamium which dated from about AD85. The cremated ashes were contained in the largest of the glass jars, while the 13 samian vessels may have been used in the funeral feast. The large iron object (back left) is the frame of a folding chair. In the foreground are two strigils, used in Roman baths, lamps, glass phials which probably held oil or perfume, and glass gaming counters used in board games. *(Copyright St Albans Museums Service).*

Fig.55. An early-3rd century lead coffin from Verulamium The moulded scallop shells were symbols of re-birth. *(Copyright St Albans Museums Service).*

the complex included a bath house, presumably used for purification rituals connected with whatever ceremonies were performed. Elsewhere in the county aristocratic graves were marked by earthen mounds or barrows, possibly continuing a pre-Roman tradition. At Stevenage a group of six barrows alongside the road from Welwyn to Baldock still provide a striking monument. All the barrows were dug into many years ago, and the finds which may have been recovered are now lost. The barrows probably date from the late first and early second centuries, and presumably belonged to members of an influential local family (fig.56). Better records survive of two further Roman barrows at Sandon, about 5 miles south-west of Braughing and some 70 yards from a villa. One was excavated in 1788 and contained spears, coins and pottery, the other was excavated by the famous Victorian archaeologist, Sir John Evans, in 1889. A 'cavity' was found in the centre of the mound, which had once contained a wooden box, about 3ft by 2ft. Within this was a burial urn containing cremated

Fig. 56. The Roman barrows at Stevenage. *(Photo - Simon West)*.

Fig. 57. The lead coffin (fig. 55) contained a remarkably well preserved skull. Using the latest forensic techniques, Richard Neave, of Manchester University, was able to reconstruct the man's appearance, giving us a unique glimpse of 'Hertfordshire Man' in the 3rd century. *(Copyright St Albans Museums Service)*.

ashes, and a large glass jar which contained a resinous substance, probably incense and perfume. There are records of further barrows at Harpenden and Munden. Only 18 *mausolea* and barrows are known from Roman Hertfordshire however, so even allowing for the fact that a large number have been destroyed, they can never have formed more than a very small proportion of the total number of burials in the county.

The human remains found in the graves give us some idea of the people themselves, and the sort of lives they lived. The process of analysing human remains is both long and costly, but information is gradually becoming available. The picture that is emerging is of a population who enjoyed a normal life expectancy for the time (about 50-60 years). On the whole they did not suffer greatly from dietary deficiencies or deliberately inflicted injuries. Although relatively robust, they led physically demanding lives and it is not surprising that they were particularly susceptible to arthritis (fig.57).

In the cemeteries at Baldock and Wheathampstead there is some evidence that graves were often grouped together, and these may well have been family grave plots, perhaps used over several generations. At Verulamium a few graves were marked with arrangements of wooden posts. It has been suggested that these are remains of shrines where offerings were made to the spirits of the dead.

Cemeteries along the Chiltern escarpment have yielded evidence of extremely bizarre burial customs which were adopted in a minority of cases, particularly in the late Roman period. Cemeteries at both Baldock and Dunstable included a small number of graves where the body had been decapitated and the skull placed at the feet or between the legs of the dead person. Why this should have been done is a mystery, but men, women and even children were occasionally buried in this way (fig.58).

Fig. 58. One of a number of graves excavated at Baldock by Gil Burleigh. In these burials the head was removed after death, and placed between the knees or at the feet of the deceased. This may have been in order to prevent the ghost returning to haunt the living. (*Copyright North Herts District Council Museums Service*).

Later History and the End of Roman Rule

A PERIOD OF PROSPERITY

After the somewhat shaky start due to the Boudiccan revolt, the period of Roman rule in Hertfordshire was, on the whole, a time of modest prosperity. The second century, in particular, saw the growth of comfortable villas, thriving villages, a number of small towns, and a large and elegant tribal centre at Verulamium. Agriculture, trade and industry flourished, profiting from a long period of peace. The only interruption to this seems to have been the fire which severely damaged Verulamium soon after 155.

At some time in the later part of the second century, or early in the third, several towns in the Catuvellaunian *civitas* were provided with defences consisting of earthen banks and ditches. Dorchester on Thames and Alcester (both in Oxfordshire) were defended in this way. The reason behind the construction of these defences is a matter of speculation, but it has been suggested that it lies in the turbulent events that overtook the empire at the very end of the second century. In AD 193, the murder of three successive Roman emperors within the space of six months led to a number of conflicting claims to the empire. Among the claimants was the governor of Britain, Clodius Albinus. Albinus was supported by the three legions stationed in Britain, and for a time he managed to maintain the position of 'Caesar' or junior partner to another aspiring emperor, Septimus Severus. By 196 however, both Severus and Albinus had determined to become the single, supreme ruler of the Roman world, and war between the two became inevitable. The following year, Albinus and a substantial part of the British garrison crossed to Gaul. The decisive battle took place at Lyons, where Albinus was defeated and Severus confirmed as emperor.

A neat and attractive explanation for the appearance of earthworks around many Romano-British towns at about this date would certainly be that Albinus had ordered their construction before withdrawing most of the garrison to support his bid for the empire. One drawback to this explanation is that it would have taken more than a few months in 196-7 to construct such defences. Furthermore, not all the earthwork defences can be dated to the end of the second century. Certainly there are no signs in Hertfordshire of any hasty defensive measures being taken. No provision was made to defend either Braughing or Baldock, while most rural settlements seem to have been unaffected by events in Gaul and in the empire as a whole.

Only in south-west Hertfordshire are there indications that some villa owners may have experienced a sharp decline in their fortunes in the early third century. One explanation could be that they had supported Albinus and, on his defeat, found that their property was confiscated by Severus. This is an intriguing possibility, but unfortunately cannot be proved. What we can say however is that whatever the reason for the early third century decline in the Verulamium area, it only affected a small proportion of the population; there is no sign of any corresponding decline elsewhere in the Catuvellaunian territory.

By AD 350 Hertfordshire had been part of the Roman empire for 300 years. The economy was based on gold, silver and bronze coins, produced by the central government to pay the army, but which percolated through the whole of provincial society. By the fourth century households up and down the county relied on factories for supplies of pottery, glassware, brick and tile, together with any food or goods not produced locally. All these were purchased with money gained from the sale of surplus local produce. Thus the whole system depended not only on good communications, but also on the maintenance of a money based economy, which in turn depended on the presence of the Roman army.

Despite the general prosperity, during the course of the Roman period the status of many of the Catuvellaunian people had changed. At the time of the conquest society was based on patterns of kinship, alongside a system of patrons and clients, whereby poorer tribesmen were supporters of, and in turn were themselves supported by, a more powerful clan leader. By the late Roman empire however this system had evolved into one of landlord and tenant; many of the poorer rural labourers were in effect tied to the land and were little better than serfs.

For most of the Roman period there was no army garrison in Hertfordshire. Even in the third century, which for much of the Roman empire was a time of considerable unrest, marked by constant warring between rival emperors, southern Britain seems to have remained at peace. Throughout the later third and fourth centuries however, there was a growing menace of attack by barbarian tribes from beyond the frontiers of the Roman empire. By the middle of the fourth century Roman Britain was being harassed from all sides; Irish raiders on the west, Picts on the north, and Saxons from northern Europe who put pressure on the east and Channel coasts. The maintenance of a garrison on Hadrian's Wall, and the presence of fleets based in large forts along the coasts, initially staved off many of these threats. In 367 however, the Picts, Irish and Saxons all attacked at the same time, and the defences of Roman Britain were overwhelmed. According to the contemporary writer Ammianus Marcellinus, it was two years before the central government was able to regain control, by which time raiders were established in the London area and had to be driven out.

These events must have had repercussions in Hertfordshire. It is difficult to imagine how the presence of barbarian raiders in London could fail to affect Verulamium, a mere 20 miles away along Watling street. Nevertheless, there is little or no sign of these troubles in the archaeological record. There is no evidence of burning or looting of property, let alone any to indicate the presence of marauding bands of Picts or Saxons. A few villas which had been successful earlier in the century (such as Gadebridge, Boxmoor and Lockleys) show signs of drastic reductions in living space in the period between about 335 and 375, but it is impossible to say whether this had anything to do with the events of 367. Nevertheless the decline of villas in the hinterland of Verulamium may be a sign of unease among the better off classes in the southern part of the county. Unlike the peasant farmers these were wealthy people who were not forced to go on living in the countryside, and it is possible that the general uncertainties of the mid-fourth century prompted them to move their families to the safety of the town, or even abroad, leaving their villas to be run by bailiffs. On the other hand it is equally possible that the villa residents in the Verulamium district had once again supported the losing political faction in one of the many political *coups* of the late Roman empire and that their estates had been confiscated as a result.

Whatever the reason, the fourth century decline in the Verulamium region was a fairly localised phenomenon which did not extend to the villas elsewhere in the county, some of which continued to prosper until the very end of the fourth century, or even later. At Bishops Stortford, a new tessellated floor was laid in the 380s, while the large villas at Little Wymondley and Radwell show little or no sign of decline in the late fourth century.

Nevertheless, at some stage in the early fifth century the entire way of life in Hertfordshire underwent a radical change, so that a century later its pattern of towns, villas and rural settlements had disappeared and it was well on its way to becoming a Saxon kingdom. The process by which this dramatic change took place remains one of the most intractable puzzles in the history of Hertfordshire.

THE COLLAPSE OF ROMAN RULE

The present state of archaeological research suggests that the initial contacts with the Saxons were gradual and peaceful. Nowhere is there any sign of burning or destruction, and such evidence as there is suggests a slow infiltration by small groups rather than massive invasions. A number of buckles and belt fittings decorated with distinctive patterns based on stylised animals have been found on several sites. At one time it was thought that these objects were part of the uniform of Germanic mercenaries who were recruited from outside the empire and settled within it to defend vulnerable areas. Doubt has now been cast on this interpretation, but the style of these buckles certainly shows pronounced affinities with Germanic styles. At the very least this suggests that by the end of the fourth century there was already an element in the local population that favoured a Germanic style of ornament.

The last decades of the fourth century were turbulent ones for Roman Britain. In 383 and 406 British usurpers made bids to become emperor of the western part of the old Roman empire. Between these two events, in 397, the province's defences were again overwhelmed and one of the empire's most experienced generals, Stilicho, crossed the Channel to retrieve the situation. Alongside these difficulties were problems caused by the repeated withdrawal of troops from Britain in order to defend various interests on the Continent. In 406 the last remnant of the army was withdrawn to the Continent to support the claims of the aspiring emperor Constantine III, never to return. The inhabitants of Roman Britain, left more or less defenceless, must have become increasingly alarmed, and in 409 they finally took responsibility for their own defences, a decision endorsed by the emperor Honorius in the following year.

The year 410 therefore effectively saw the end of direct Roman rule in Britain, although some contacts, particularly those concerning the church, were maintained. With the final departure of the last of the Roman army in 406, the new supplies of coins with which it had been paid ceased to come into the country, with the consequence that trade quickly collapsed.

The road network also decayed. Some Hertfordshire roads were already in disrepair; the road north of Verulamium and Ermine street at Ware were both progressively encroached upon by roadside shacks during the fourth century, and by the end of the Roman period were pitted with pot holes and rubbish pits. As military establishments along the Channel coast ceased to be maintained, so trade with the Continent must have become increasingly hazardous, while the weakening of central authority may have led to an increase in unrest in the countryside. All these factors contributed to a dramatic decline in trade, and with it the collapse of the large scale industries, particularly that of pottery and tile manufacture, so important to the economy of Roman Hertfordshire.

The disappearance both of pottery and coins brings particular problems for any archaeologist dealing with the end of the Romano-British period. Without either pottery or coins it is extremely difficult to give a precise date to any remains that are found. Added to this, the decline in tile and brick manufacture means that the latest buildings in Roman Hertfordshire were built not of masonry and mortar, but of timber. Their remains are far less substantial than those of their predecessors, while at the same time they are less deeply buried and so were more vulnerable to later disturbances; many late Roman wooden buildings must have been totally ploughed away.

Fig.59. Imaginative reconstruction of a 5th century house in the centre of Verulamium. *(Drawn by Clare Pollak).*

With the general run down in trade, the local population must have had to become almost entirely self-sufficient, and, as they increasingly had to rely on subsistence farming to make ends meet, so villas fell into disrepair and towns shrank in size.

VERULAMIUM

By the fifth century the town was reverting to something like its pre-Roman origins. A local social elite probably continued to live in a few large, aristocratic mansions, surrounded by areas of market gardens and small-holdings. Corn, grown in the surrounding district, was brought into the town to be processed and stored. Two sizeable barns and several large corn-drying ovens are known, all apparently late Roman in date. By the late fourth century the theatre was no longer used, and instead it was filled with rubbish tips. It is not known whether the forum was still functioning at this period, but in the area between it and the theatre two masonry houses were still being occupied (fig.59). One of these houses was a large mansion with at least 20 rooms, in one of which a fine new mosaic was laid at the very end of the fourth century. The house subsequently underwent further alterations, and over the years the mosaic became heavily worn before it was finally replaced by a large corn-drying oven. The oven itself was later replaced by a stone built barn, which in its turn was demolished and a new water pipe, supplying the central area of Verulamium with fresh running water, was laid over it. The absence both of pottery and coins makes precise dating difficult, but the provision of the new water main must date to about the middle of the fifth century, if not later. Of course, this continued activity may only relate to one or two wealthy households operating near the centre of the old town, so town life in any real sense may have ceased to be maintained.

Verulamium however was unusual, if not unique, in that it was the centre for an important Christian shrine. In AD 429, the Bishop of Auxerre, St Germanus, crossed to Britain in order to combat a heresy, the Pelagian heresy, which was particularly strong in Britain. In the course of his visit, Germanus went to St Alban's shrine and apparently found Verulamium thriving. Occasional finds of fifth and sixth century metalwork in the area around St Albans Abbey remind us of the possibility that the shrine continued to be venerated as a place of pilgrimage throughout the so called 'Dark Ages' The famous Anglian historian, Bede, writing in 731, tells us that in his day a Roman church was still in existence on the site of St Alban's grave and martyrdom.

HERTFORDSHIRE IN THE FIFTH CENTURY

Elsewhere in Hertfordshire the change from Roman province to Saxon kingdom proceeded rather differently. From the early fifth century onwards groups of Saxons established themselves along the Chiltern escarpment. At Luton and Kempston (both just outside the modern county boundary) cemeteries have been excavated which included graves containing brooches of unmistakably Saxon workmanship dating from the early fifth century. A similarly early burial has been recorded on the north of the county at Ashwell. While it is possible that the brooches were old when they were placed in the graves (perhaps they were family heirlooms), together they are surely evidence for Saxon infiltrations along the Icknield Way in the course of the fifth century. The distribution and style of the earliest Saxon brooches in Buckinghamshire, Oxfordshire and Hertfordshire suggests that this infiltration was carried out by groups moving north from the Thames valley, rather than south from the Wash.

As in earlier years, there is no sign of violent clashes in the wake of this infiltration. At Pirton, just outside Hitchin, a rural settlement that had been first established 500 years previously continued in uninterrupted occupation up until the seventh century. On the other hand there is a distinct impression that the population in Hertfordshire suffered a severe decline. Although in places like Pirton occupation may have persisted, many other sites were certainly abandoned. At Baldock and Welwyn, the discovery of the remains of wild animals in the latest archaeological levels has been seen as evidence for deserted, ruinous sites, where deer and foxes roamed, occasionally falling into open well shafts, or becoming trapped beneath falling buildings. Such interpretations are surely evocative of a depleted population and the desertion of once thriving settlements. A rather unreliable fifth century British writer, Gildas, mentions a severe plague afflicting the British in the early fifth century, and we cannot altogether discount the possibility that natural disasters, such as a succession of bad harvests or a disastrous epidemic, played as large a part in the abrupt decline of Roman Hertfordshire as did the advent of hostile settlers.

Places to Visit

(Information is correct at the time of writing. Details, particularly opening hours, may change.)

ASHWELL VILLAGE MUSEUM
This museum of local history and village life includes displays of Roman pottery, a cremation burial and coins.
Open: 2.30-5 pm, Sundays and Bank Holidays. Entrance Fee.
Tel (01462) 742956

BISHOPS STORTFORD MUSEUM
The local society museum, in the grounds of the cemetery, includes a small display of finds from Roman sites in the area.
Open: May-Sept, 2-5 pm, Fridays and 1st Sunday of month.
Tel (01279) 722557

BRITISH MUSEUM
Several important finds of Iron Age and Roman material from Hertfordshire are on display in the British Museum in London. These include two chieftain's burials from Welwyn and Welwyn Garden City, painted wall plaster from Roman Verulamium and the hoard of Romano-British bronze and silver objects from Barkway.

CHILTERN OPEN AIR MUSEUM
An Iron Age house is among buildings which have been restored and reconstructed just outside the county boundary at Newlands Park, Chalfont St Giles.
Open: April-Oct, 2-6 pm, Wed-Sun and Bank Holidays. Entrance Fee.
Tel (01494) 872163

ERMINE STREET
A public trackway and bridleway (Elbow Lane) follows a two mile stretch of the Roman road south from Hertford Heath (fig.12). The ditches on either side of the road are recent, but the walk gives a good idea of what a major Roman road must have been like. Access from the B1197 at Hertford Heath (between Hertford and Hoddesdon), or from lanes to the west of Hoddesdon.

HATFIELD MILL GREEN MUSEUM

The museum is housed in the mill house of a historic water mill on the river Lea, which has been restored to working order. The museum displays the history of the area, and includes displays of late Iron Age and Roman material from Welwyn and Essendon.

Open: 10 am-5 pm, Tues-Fri; 2-5 pm, Sat, Sun, Bank Holidays.
Tel (01707) 271362

HODDESDON LOWEWOOD MUSEUM

A small museum displaying collections from the Broxbourne area, including a small amount of material from Roman Cheshunt.

Open: 10 am-4 pm, Wed and Sat.
Tel (01992) 445596

ICKNIELD WAY

This ancient ridgeway now has a waymarked long distance footpath, running along the northern edge of the county from Tring to Royston. It forms part of the longer path which can be followed from Wiltshire to Norfolk. A good stretch of the path can be reached from a car park on the B655, 3 miles west of Hitchin, near Deacon Hill.

LETCHWORTH MUSEUM

The museum is in the town centre and has displays dealing with natural history, archaeology and local history. The displays of Iron Age and Roman material from the area are particularly rich and include the finds from the Baldock chieftain's burial.

Open: 10 am-5 pm, Mon-Sat.
Tel (01462) 685647

LYNCHETS

There are two places in the county where lynchets (ancient field banks) can be clearly seen. The exact date of these features is uncertain, but they may have started to form in the late Iron Age or Roman periods.

One set of lynchets is on the Chiltern escarpment about a mile southwest of Pirton. They can be seen from the Icknield footpath between Pirton and Deacon Hill, in the Knocking Hoe dry valley, just below the top of the ridge about 600 yards north of the B655.

An impressive series of lynchets can also be seen on the north slope of the Chess valley between Sarratt and Latimer. The actual date of these lynchets is not certain, and it is possible that they were formed in the Middle Ages. On the other hand, there are a number of Roman sites in the area, and the lynchets may have started to build up in the Roman period.

REDBOURN; THE AUBREYS HILL FORT

The bank and ditch defences of this Iron Age hill fort (fig.3) lie in the grounds of the Aubrey Park Hotel, which stands on the west side of the M1, where the B487 from Redbourn to Hemel Hempstead passes under the motorway. There is a Hertfordshire County Council information board on the site, and the bank and ditch can be seen from a footpath which passes in front of the hotel.

STEVENAGE MUSEUM

The museum display includes coins and pottery from Roman sites in the area.
Open: 10 am-5 pm, Mon-Sat (closed Bank Holidays).
Tel (01438) 354292

STEVENAGE: SIX HILLS ROMAN BARROWS

The six Roman burial mounds (fig.56) are preserved near the centre of Stevenage on the west side of the B197, 500 yards south of Stevenage Station. There is a Hertfordshire County Council information board on the site which describes the barrows.

ST ALBANS: BEECH BOTTOM DYKE

A massive bank and ditch dating from the first century AD and forming part of a territorial boundary can be followed for a mile. A public footpath runs along the eastern side of the earthwork. Access is from the Harpenden road (the A1081) immediately north east of the junction with the northern ring road opposite the Ancient Briton Public House.

ST ALBANS VERULAMIUM MUSEUM

The Verulamium Museum contains major displays of material illustrating life in the Roman town of Verulamium and its late Iron Age predecessor. Mosaics and wall plaster from the town are on show, as well as numerous finds recreating every day life.
Open: (April-Sept) 10 am-5 30 pm, Mon-Sat; 2-5.30 pm, Sun; (Oct-Mar) 10 am-4.30 pm, Mon-Sat. Entrance Fee.
Tel (01727) 819339

ST ALBANS: VERULAMIUM PARK

Remains of the Roman town wall (fig.26) are visible in the Park, as are the foundations of the south-east gate into the town (the London Gate). One of the bastions, projecting from the town wall, can be seen near the south corner of the park, close to the footpath leading to King Harry Lane. A sign post in the Verulamium Museum car park directs visitors to a small 1950s building in the centre of the park which houses a second century mosaic floor with an intact hypocaust (under-floor heating system). The original Roman painted wall plaster has been recreated on the interior. The building is open during Verulamium Museum opening hours.

ST ALBANS: VERULAMIUM THEATRE
The remains of the only visible Roman theatre in Britain (front cover and fig. 17) are privately owned and lie in the Gorhambury Estate, on the other side of the A4147 from the Verulamium Museum and car park. Adjoining the theatre are the foundations of Roman shops and part of the third century underground shrine.
Open: Summer 10 am-5 pm, Winter 10 am-4 pm. Entrance Fee.
Tel (01727) 835035

WARE MUSEUM
A small museum in the centre of Ware. The displays illustrate the history of Ware and include material from the Roman settlement, including a Roman slave chain, and illustrations of local excavations.
Open: Summer 11 am-5 pm, Sat; 2-4pm, Sun; Winter 11 am-4 pm, Sat; 2-4 pm, Sun.
Tel (01920) 487848

WATFORD MUSEUM
The museum is housed in a former brewery and has collections that deal largely with the local industries of brewing, printing and paper making. There is a small display of Roman material from local sites.
Open: 10 am-5 pm, Mon-Fri; 10 am-1pm and 2-5 pm, Sat.
Tel (01923) 232297

WELWYN: ROMAN BATH HOUSE
The remains of a bath house, (fig.40) attached to the Dicket Mead villa, have been preserved beneath a steel vault under the A1(M) close to the village of old Welwyn. The remains are approached through a short tunnel and are complemented by very informative displays of material from the site and interpretative panels. The site is managed by the Mill Green Museum, Hatfield.
Open: 2-5 pm, Thur-Sun and Bank Holidays. Entrance Fee.
Tel (01707) 271362

WHEATHAMPSTEAD: DEVILS DYKE
The impressive earthworks forming the west side of the pre-Roman stronghold (fig.2) can be seen by walking up the public footpath alongside Dyke Road, which leads south from the road to Welwyn on the eastern outskirts of Wheathampstead.

Further Reading

An excellent, up to date and well illustrated general account of Roman Britain is *The Oxford Illustrated History of Roman Britain*, Peter Salway. Oxford, 1993. Another authoritative account of the history and development of the province is *Britannia: A History of Roman Britain* by S. S. Frere, 3rd edition, London 1987.

For the pre-Roman background *Iron Age Communities in Britain* by B. W. Cunliffe, 3rd edition, London, 1991, provides the standard account, while *The Celts* by T. G. E. Powell, London, 1980, deals with the Celtic peoples of western Europe as a whole.

There are no modern books specifically dealing with Roman Hertfordshire, but *The Catuvellauni* by Keith Branigan, Sutton, 1985, provides a comprehensive account of the tribal territory as a whole, which included Buckinghamshire, Middlesex and parts of Oxfordshire, Northamptonshire and Cambridgeshire. *The Archaeology of the Chilterns* edited by Keith Branigan and published in 1994 by the Chess Valley Archaeological Society covers local archaeology from the last Ice Age until the Saxon period, and contains much information on Roman Hertfordshire, as does *Recent Archaeological Research in the Chilterns*, a collection of short papers on archaeological topics edited by R. Holgate and which is due to be published by The Book Castle, Dunstable, in 1995. Articles and papers on a variety of archaeological and historical topics relating to Hertfordshire are published in *Hertfordshire Archaeology*, which is produced jointly by the two major archaeological societies in the county, the East Hertfordshire Archaeological Society and the St Albans and Hertfordshire Archaeological and Architectural Society. *Hertfordshire Archaeology* is available in public libraries in the county.

Detailed accounts of excavations in Verulamium in the 1950s and early 1960s can be found in *Verulamium Excavations, volumes I-III* by S. S. Frere, which were published in 1972 (volume I), 1983 (volume II) and 1984 (volume III). The first two volumes were published by the Society of Antiquaries of London, and the third by the Oxford University Press. Accounts of the small towns at Baldock and Braughing can be found in *The "Small Towns" of Roman Britain* by B. C. Burnham and J. S. Wacher, London, 1990. General discussions of Romano-British villas and the countryside in Roman Britain are contained in *Studies in the*

Romano-British Villa edited by M. Todd, Leicester, 1978, and *Villas in Roman Britain* edited by Keith Branigan and David Miles, Sheffield, 1991. For definitive accounts of the excavation of two Hertfordshire villas see *The Excavation of a Roman Villa in Gadebridge Park*, (London, 1974) and *Excavation of the Iron Age, Roman and Medieval Settlement at Gorhambury, St Albans* (London, 1990), both by David Neal. *Foxholes Farm: A Multi-Period Gravel Site* by Clive Partridge is a definitive report on the excavation of the Romano-British rural site at Foxholes Farm, near Hertford; it was published by the Hertfordshire Archaeological Trust in 1989. The classic account of Roman roads remains I. D. Margary's *Roman Roads in Britain* (London, 1967). More detailed discussion of possible road routes in Hertfordshire can be found in *Roman Roads in the South-East Midlands* by the Viatores, (London, 1964), although not all the routes suggested in it are certain.

For particular aspects of Romano-British life see *The Gods of the Celts* (Gloucester, 1986) by Miranda Green, *Religion in Roman Britain* (London, 1984) by Martin Henig and *Women in Roman Britain* (London, 1989) by L. Allason-Jones. These are all excellent general accounts of particular topics.

Index